# Regeneration

Study Guide by Course Hero

## What's Inside

## 👁 Book Basics

### AUTHOR
Pat Barker

### YEAR PUBLISHED
1991

### GENRE
War Literature

### PERSPECTIVE AND NARRATOR
*Regeneration* is narrated in the third person by an omniscient narrator.

### TENSE
*Regeneration* is narrated in the past tense.

### ABOUT THE TITLE
*Regeneration* refers to a treatment method used on traumatized soldiers and officers at a military hospital in Scotland during World War I (1914–18). The book's protagonist, Dr. W.H.R. Rivers, based on a real and well-known medical figure of the time, helps patients bring memories of traumatic experiences into their conscious minds so they can become free of them and regenerate their mental and physical health.

## ⊘ In Context

## Britain in World War I

The characters in this book are soldiers or officers who fought in the British armed forces in World War I (1914–18). The book explores how the experience of war has affected them both physically and psychologically.

After a long period of relative peace during the 19th century, Europe maintained an effective balance of power among the major countries until about 1907, when Germany began flexing its military muscle by building up its armed forces and gearing its economy increasingly toward the military. To counter the rise of German power, Britain joined France and Russia in an alliance called the Triple Entente, an agreement for mutual support but not necessarily military defense if one of the Entente nations were attacked by Germany or another aggressor.

The event that precipitated the war was the assassination of the Austro-Hungarian Archduke Ferdinand in Sarajevo in June 1914. However, that event may be viewed as a pretext, or excuse, for prosecuting the war that followed. The actual cause of the war remains elusive and uncertain—and is still debated among historians. In her fine history of the First World War, *The War That Ended Peace* (2013), Canadian historian Margaret MacMillan wrote: "We also remember the Great War because it is such a puzzle. How could Europe have done this to itself and to the world? There are many possible explanations; indeed, so many that it is difficult to choose among them. For a start the arms race ... economic rivalry, trade wars, imperialism ... nationalism with its unsavory riders of hatred and contempt for others ... the demands of honor and manliness which meant not backing down or appearing weak ... The military as the noblest part of the nation and the spread of military values into civilian societies fed the assumptions that war was a necessary part of the great struggle for survival ... It was [also] Europe's and the world's tragedy in retrospect that none of the key players in 1914 were great and imaginative leaders who had the courage to stand out against the pressures building up for war." MacMillan quotes the British politician and prime minister (1916–1922) David Lloyd George (1863–1945) who said, "The nations slithered over the brink into the boiling cauldron of war without any trace of apprehension or dismay."

On the nights of August 3–4, 1914, German forces heading to France invaded the neutral nation of Belgium. The British government intervened in accordance with the Treaty of London (1839), in which Britain promised to defend Belgium against foreign aggression. Debate raged in the British Parliament about whether to declare war on Germany for invading Belgium. But on August 4, 1914, when German troops began moving out of Belgium to attack France, Britain acted and declared war. In only a few days, France and Russia joined Britain, as the Allies, in war against Germany. Most people on both sides of the conflict believed that World War I (1914–18), the setting of the novel, would be over in a matter of months.

At the start of the war, Britain had only about 250,000 men in arms, but by the end of 1914, more than one million men had enlisted to fight in the war. By December 1915 that number grew to more than 2.5 million. In total about 5.2 million British soldiers fought in World War I. Between one and two million were fighting on the Western Front—roughly the border region between France and Germany and Belgium and Germany—at any one time during the war.

## The Fighting

*Regeneration* describes the appalling circumstances these soldiers faced on the Western Front. Soldiers lived in tunnel-like trenches, filled with lice, rats, and mud. The enemy lived in similar trenches some short distance away. In between was an area known as "No Man's Land," filled with dead trees, dead soldiers, and craters where bombs had exploded. Some bombs fell in trenches and killed soldiers there. When the military brass gave the order, soldiers climbed out of their trenches—known as going "over the top"—and charged across No Man's Land toward enemy lines. Usually the enemy soldiers in the opposing trenches had their rifles ready and cut down the soldiers who charged directly into the line of fire. If a large enough force of charging soldiers survived No Man's Land, they might kill—by gunfire or bayonet—enemy soldiers in their trenches or force the enemy soldiers to abandon their trench and retreat. Thus a huge number of soldiers sacrificed their lives to gain, at most, a few hundred meters of territory. World War I is also notable as the first war in which poison gas, such as mustard gas and chlorine gas, was used as a deadly weapon, vastly increasing the number of casualties.

As historian Vanda Wilcox writes, "The men and women who served in the First World War endured some of the most brutal forms of warfare ever known. Millions were sent to fight away from home for months, even years at a time, and underwent a series of terrible physical and emotional experiences." Ernest Hemingway, the great American novelist and a World War I veteran, wrote: "There were many words that you could not stand to hear and finally only the names of places had dignity ... Abstract words such as glory, honor, courage, or hallow were obscene." The characters in this book carry the scars of these horrific experiences, and the process of healing (when possible) is an important topic in the novel.

## Casualties

The patient-soldiers in this novel are casualties of the fighting in France during World War I. British casualties were enormous, as were casualties for most armies. July 1, 1916, the first day of the Battle of the Somme in France, is remembered as "the worst day in British army history," with 57,470 casualties. By the time the Battle of the Somme ended, in November 1916, the British had suffered more than 420,000 casualties. At the Battle of Passchendaele, in Belgium, between July 31 and November 6, 1917, Britain suffered about

217,000 casualties and gained very little territory. As a result "Passchendaele" became a symbol of the war's horrors and wasted lives.

By war's end, of the 8,904,467 soldiers mobilized from the British Empire, 908,371 were killed, nearly 2.1 million were injured, and about 192,000 were missing in action or taken prisoner, totaling 35.8 percent of all forces mobilized.

# British Women in World War I

Before World War I between 11 and 13 percent of working-age women in England and Wales worked as domestic servants. By 1931 the number dropped to less than 8 percent. As millions of men left for the front, British women took over many of their jobs. In 1911, 33,000 women worked for the British civil service; by 1912 this number soared to 102,000.

Women, such as those in this novel, began working in munitions factories in 1915. By 1918 more than a million British women were working in such factories. Many of these women worked with the explosive TNT, which often caused toxic jaundice, a potentially fatal disease whose clearest symptom was yellow skin. An estimated 400 British women suffered from toxic jaundice during the war years; a quarter of these cases were fatal.

Women working in factories during the war were almost always paid less than the men they replaced. Some women workers went on strike for wage parity—a goal women still fight for today.

# Craiglockhart War Hospital

The men portrayed in *Regeneration* are a tiny fraction of the more than two million who were injured and returned home to Britain with serious physical or mental traumas. Craiglockhart War Hospital, near Edinburgh, Scotland, was opened as a "shell shock" military hospital for treating soldiers mentally or physically scarred during the Battle of the Somme in France (1916, World War I battle fought between the British and French Empires against the German Empire). The novel is set at Craiglockhart Hospital, where soldiers suffering the psychological effects of their traumatic war experiences (then called shell shock) were treated. Shell shock is often today referred to as post-traumatic stress disorder, or PTSD. PTSD

is a mental health condition that some people develop after experiencing or witnessing a life-threatening event, as often happens in combat.

The hospital's staff became famous for their approach to neuropsychiatry championed by Dr. W.H.R. Rivers—the protagonist of *Regeneration*. Neuropsychiatry is psychiatry that relates mental or emotional problems to disordered brain function. Physical and mental breakdowns were believed to result from severe psychological stresses, such as those experienced during war. Craiglockhart is one of the few hospitals of its type that retained records of the soldiers treated there. According to these records, of the 1,736 patients the hospital treated between October 1916 and March 1919, 735 were listed as "discharged, medically unfit." Another 89 soldiers were put on "home service"—working for the military from their home country; 141 were transferred to other medical facilities; and 758 were released and returned to combat.

Aside from Dr. Rivers's innovative and frequently effective treatment of soldiers with war neurosis, or breakdown, Craiglockhart is also known as the place where two of Britain's most gifted poets of the 20th century met and became close friends.

# Sassoon and Owen

The English poets featured in the novel, Siegfried Sassoon and Wilfred Owen, met while both were being treated for traumatic breakdown at Craiglockhart. Both were second lieutenants in the British army when they arrived at the hospital. At the time they met, Sassoon was already fairly well known, and some of his poetry had been published. Sassoon was astute enough to recognize in Owen a brilliant poetic talent; many would come to consider Owen the greatest poet of the World War I era. Sassoon became a friend and mentor to Owen, who was somewhat awed by the rich, famous, and talented Sassoon. Owen had already read many of Sassoon's published poems, and he greatly admired Sassoon's poetic gift.

At Craiglockhart Owen became more committed to Sassoon's opposition to the war, as delineated in Sassoon's Declaration of July 1917 that he was opposed to any further fighting. Both men felt an immense responsibility for the soldiers they'd left behind in France. Both poets may well have secured a home-service recommendation from Craiglockhart and spent the rest of the war working for the military in Britain. But they wanted to help their comrades who were suffering on the front lines, so both returned to the fighting.

Sassoon survived World War I and died in 1967. Owen met a more tragic fate. He chose to return to the front after treatment at Craiglockhart. He was killed in combat in northern France on November 4, 1918, one week before the war ended and an Armistice was declared.

# Author Biography

## Early Life

Pat Barker was born in Thornaby-on-Tees in Yorkshire in northern England on May 8, 1943. Barker was born to a single mother, Moyra, and raised in a working-class family. Barker's mother and grandmother were housekeepers and the family's only breadwinners. When Barker was seven, her mother left the family home to get married, but Barker chose to stay and be raised by her grandparents because she did not get along with her stepfather.

Barker's mother claimed Barker's biological father was killed during World War II (1939–45), yet Barker continued to imagine he was still alive and hoped he and her mother would reunite. As an adult Barker has said her mother told a lot of "incredible stories" about her father. When Barker's mother was on her deathbed, Barker learned her mother had never known the identity of Barker's father.

Although her early life was difficult economically and personally, Barker was much loved by her grandparents. As a youngster she helped her grandparents run their fish-and-chip shop, wrapping up meals in newspapers. She became an avid newspaper reader, and her grandmother encouraged her to do well in school. After completing high school, Barker attended the London School of Economics where she studied international history. She later attended Durham University.

In 1969 she met David Barker, a professor and neurologist 20 years her senior. They married in 1978 and had two children. David Barker encouraged and supported his wife's ambition to be a writer.

## Becoming a Writer

Barker began to write when she was in her mid-20s. Her first three novels were never published. Barker admits they "didn't deserve to be." Her first published novels describe the difficult lives of working-class women in northern England. The first of these, *Union Street* (1982), won the Fawcett Society Book Prize. In 1983 Barker was named among the Twenty Best Young British Novelists. Her second novel, *Blow Your House Down* (1984), was adapted into a successful stage play. Other novels followed, such as *The Century's Daughter* (1986; published in the United States as *Liza's England* in 1996) and *The Man Who Wasn't There* (1989).

## World War I Novels

Barker was inspired to write about World War I by her grandfather, who fought in the trenches of France. He acquired a serious bayonet scar that he had for the rest of his life. The first novel in her World War I trilogy, *Regeneration* (1991), won high praise. A film version released in 1997 was originally given the same name but later retitled *Behind the Lines*. The novels *Eye in the Door* (1993) and *The Ghost Road* (1995) complete the trilogy. *The Ghost Road* was awarded the highly prestigious Man Booker Prize for Fiction in 1995.

Barker has said her World War I novels can make for difficult reading because she tackles distressing subjects directly. Her vulnerable characters and the horrific wartime experiences they endure make these works emotionally wrenching as well as engrossing and deeply humane.

# Characters

## Dr. Rivers

Dr. Rivers is a compassionate doctor, who helps traumatized soldiers remember and recover from their war experiences. Although he helps many, he is conflicted about his work. After his patients recover, he is duty bound to recommend their return to the war—a war he comes to oppose.

# Siegfried Sassoon

Siegfried Sassoon is a rich, aristocratic army officer and talented poet; he lands at Craiglockhart after he writes a Declaration in fierce condemnation of the war. War supporters want to keep Sassoon at the hospital so he can't publicize his views. Eventually Sassoon returns to the war out of a sense of duty, but he never changes his views about it.

# Billy Prior

Billy Prior is a young working-class man, who was promoted to an officer's rank when he served at the front. He arrives at Craiglockhart after war traumas leave him temporarily mute. Prior is intelligent, sharp-witted, and acutely aware of class bigotry in Britain. While Rivers treats him, Prior challenges and questions the psychiatrist at every turn—sometimes just for the pleasure he derives from doing so.

# Wilfred Owen

Wilfred Owen is a young and fairly innocent soldier, as well as a brilliant poet. At Craiglockhart Owen is treated for the stammer he developed at the front. Owen edits the hospital's patient publication and meets Sassoon, who becomes his mentor. Sassoon encourages Owen to polish, and publish, some of his most searing poems against the conflict.

# David Burns

David Burns is a young officer sent to Craiglockhart for treatment. Dr. Rivers tries to help him but has little success. Burns is too stressed to speak about his terrible war experiences; his reticence prevents him from releasing his memories and recovering. Unable to eat, he is gaunt and emaciated, like a "fossilized schoolboy."

# Anderson

Anderson is a trained surgeon, who worked at frontline hospitals during the war. His experience has left him unable to tolerate the sight of blood. Anderson is tormented not only by his traumatic experience at the front but also by worries about whether he'll be able to resume his career.

# Sarah Lumb

Sarah Lumb is an outspoken and tough-minded working-class woman who works in a munitions factory. Like her mother, Sarah is keenly aware of the limitations placed on women of her class and the problems they often have to live with, especially those involving men. After she meets Billy Prior, the two seem to form a mutually supportive relationship.

# Character Map

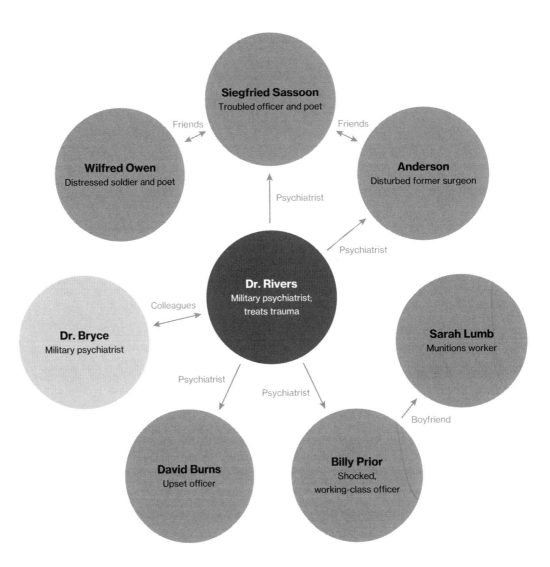

● Main Character

● Other Major Character

● Minor Character

# Full Character List

| Character | Description |
| --- | --- |
| Dr. Rivers | Dr. W.H.R. Rivers is a psychiatrist at Craiglockhart War Hospital. |
| Siegfried Sassoon | Siegfried Sassoon, an upper-class, anti-war military officer and gifted poet, is a patient at Craiglockhart War Hospital. |
| Billy Prior | Billy Prior is a working-class officer sent to Craiglockhart War Hospital because of the traumas he experienced on the battlefield; he arrives mute but regains his voice under Dr. Rivers's care. He is a fictitious character in the book, unlike the other men who were real historical figures. |
| Wilfred Owen | Wilfred Owen is a young poet and soldier sent to Craiglockhart War Hospital for trauma treatment. |
| David Burns | David Burns is a young officer sent to Craiglockhart War Hospital after a terrible war trauma leaves him unable to eat or to speak about his experience. |
| Anderson | Anderson, a trained surgeon, is sent to Craiglockhart War Hospital for treatment after he is traumatized by working at frontline hospitals. |
| Sarah Lumb | Sarah Lumb is a working-class munitions worker who becomes Billy Prior's girlfriend. |
| Betty | Betty is one of Sarah Lumb's coworkers at the munitions factory. After she gets pregnant, she tries to abort the baby with a coat hanger. |
| Dr. Bryce | Dr. Bryce is a psychiatrist at Craiglockhart War Hospital; he is Rivers's boss and friend. |
| Callan | Callan, a soldier who has taken part in many major battles, becomes Dr. Yealland's patient at the National Hospital after war trauma leaves him mute. |
| Featherstone | Featherstone is Prior's sleep-deprived roommate at Craiglockhart War Hospital. |
| Fothersgill | Fothersgill is Sassoon's roommate at Craiglockhart War Hospital. He is a religious fanatic who talks as if he's from the Middle Ages. |
| Robert Graves | Robert Graves is an upper-class poet, soldier, and friend of Sassoon's. Although he opposes World War I, he refuses to speak out against it. |
| Henry Head | Henry Head is a psychiatrist who attended Cambridge with Rivers; they researched nerve regeneration together at the college. The two remain good friends. |
| Major Huntley | Major Huntley is an openly bigoted Board member at Craiglockhart War Hospital. |
| John Layard | John Layard is one of Rivers's former patients; Rivers sees similarities between Billy Prior, a current patient, and Layard. |
| Lizzie | Lizzie is Sarah Lumb's friend and fellow munitions worker. |
| Ada Lumb | Ada Lumb is Sarah Lumb's mother. She worries Sarah may get pregnant and wants her daughter to think of financial stability rather than romance. |
| Madge | Madge is one of Sarah Lumb's coworkers at the munitions factory. |
| Peter | Peter, a soldier acquainted with both Graves and Sassoon, is arrested for soliciting male sex near a barracks and must undergo psychiatric treatment. |

| | |
|---|---|
| Mr. Prior | Mr. Prior, Billy Prior's father, is a working-class man who thinks Billy should know his place and stay there. |
| Mrs. Prior | Mrs. Prior, Billy Prior's mother, is quite unlike her husband; she thinks Billy should keep striving to better himself and rise out of the working class. |
| Pugh | Pugh is a patient at Craiglockhart War Hospital who is severely mentally wounded because of a grenade accident that killed everyone else in his platoon. |
| Thorpe | Thorpe is a patient at Craiglockhart War Hospital whose war traumas have left him with a severe stutter. |
| Willard | Willard, a patient at Craiglockhart War Hospital, is a soldier whose traumatic war experience has left him unable to walk. |
| Dr. Lewis Yealland | Dr. Lewis Yealland works at the National Hospital in London, where he treats traumatized soldiers with electroshock therapy. |

# ⌁ Plot Summary

As a novel, this book is a work of fiction even though the author includes people who actually lived through the war (Dr. Rivers, Dr. Yealland, and the poets Sassoon and Owen, for example). The author fictionalizes the stories of these actual people by imagining and writing about what their lives and interactions may have been like.

## Rivers and Sassoon

The novel begins with a letter, or Declaration, written by British poet Siegfried Sassoon, in which he explains his opposition to World War I. The letter, published in a London newspaper in July 1917, sets out Sassoon's critique of the callous individuals behind the war, who demand the sacrifice of men in a pointless, meaningless cause. The letter has upset the British military leadership, so they send Sassoon to Craiglockhart War

Hospital, near Edinburgh, Scotland, for treatment. The hospital treats British soldiers suffering from disorders, often psychological, arising from war trauma. Rather than court-martial (to be subjected to military trial) the famous poet, the military brass decide his opposition to the war is a symptom of Sassoon's mental instability. His stay at Craiglockhart is intended to "cure" him of his anti-war stance and get him back to the war front as a British officer.

Psychiatrist W.H.R. Rivers treats Sassoon at Craiglockhart. Dr. Rivers encourages Sassoon and other soldiers to talk about their war experiences—a treatment intended to heal those whose minds have been shattered by the war. The ultimate goal is to send these soldiers back to the battlefield. Despite his dedication to his task, Rivers empathizes strongly with the soldiers' horrific battle traumas.

Although Rivers and Sassoon get along well, one of the conflicts running through the novel is Rivers's mandate to convince Sassoon to return to France to fight. Sassoon, on the other hand, is intent on being court-martialed so he can publicize his anti-war Declaration.

Rivers treats an array of soldiers suffering the effects of war. David Burns is unable to eat; Anderson, a former surgeon, cannot abide the sight of blood; Billy Prior is unable to speak. Rivers suffers symptoms too, resulting from the stress and moral conflicts of his work. Like many of the soldiers and officers at Craiglockhart, he has terrible nightmares. One of the first described in the novel relates to nerve-regeneration experiments Rivers did with a colleague, Henry Head, years before. The pain he caused Head during the experiments haunts Rivers.

Sassoon's Declaration is read in the British House of Commons, but its viewpoint is discounted and its author deemed mentally unstable. Sassoon anticipated this response, yet he is still disappointed. He begins to realize he will never be court-martialed. When he meets poet and traumatized soldier Wilfred Owen at the hospital, Sassoon becomes more involved in writing poetry, and the two men become friends.

## Return to the World and to

# Duty

As Rivers treats Prior, the young working-class soldier who has lost his ability to speak, Prior gradually improves and is allowed to walk outside the hospital grounds. On a trip to an Edinburgh pub, he meets Sarah Lumb, who works in a munitions factory. She and Prior begin going out together. On occasions when they are among many civilians, Prior is overwhelmed with resentment toward those who have managed to avoid serving in the war.

Prior implores Rivers to hypnotize him to help him release his repressed memories of the war. Rivers agrees despite some skepticism. The hypnosis works, enabling Prior to remember his traumatic experiences on the battlefield.

One night Rivers is awakened by chest pain. Another Craiglockhart doctor diagnoses overwork and stress as the cause, and he insists Rivers take a three-week vacation. Rivers takes time to visit his brother, and then he spends some time with Henry Head, who offers Rivers a job at a London war hospital. Rivers says he'll think about it. Rivers then spends some time at Burns's home in the English countryside. Burns has been discharged from military service, but he is still suffering from his war trauma. At one point he attempts suicide, but Rivers saves him.

Board members who determine the fate of soldiers treated at Craiglockhart decide Prior can be assigned to permanent home service, which means he doesn't have to return to the front and the fighting. When Prior tells Sarah, she is happy for him but unsure about their relationship. Sarah and Prior decide to continue to see each other to see how their relationship develops.

Meanwhile, Sassoon has been conflicted about his future. After realizing the military won't court-martial him—since they don't want his Declaration to be made public—he decides to return to France and aid the British men fighting there. He especially wants to lead and care for the men in his battalion. He feels he cannot now abandon them by staying in Britain. Rivers is glad Sassoon has chosen to return to the fighting, although both, of course, are aware of the dangers.

# A Different Type of Treatment

Dr. Lewis Yealland at National Hospital in London invites Rivers to witness his own method for "curing" the soldiers in his care. Yealland's method is electroshock; a horrified Rivers observes Yealland using the shock treatment to achieve quick results with a mute soldier named Callan. Yealland's indifference and inhumanity toward the soldiers contrasts sharply with Rivers's far more humane, empathic approach. That night Rivers has a terrible nightmare in which he seems to be torturing a soldier in a manner similar to Yealland's. Rivers realizes that, even though he is more humane toward the soldiers, both he and Yealland have the same inhumane goal—to "cure" soldiers so they can return to the horrors of a senseless war. Rivers decides to join Yealland at National Hospital.

Rivers briefly returns to Craiglockhart to sit on the Board that decides the patients' fate. The Board grants Dr. Anderson a desk job with the military. Sassoon is allowed to return to France to fight. As Rivers prepares to return to London he says goodbye to Sassoon. Rivers realizes that Sassoon, Prior, and the other soldiers, men he was to have changed and cured, have, in fact, forever changed him and his attitude toward the war.

# Plot Diagram

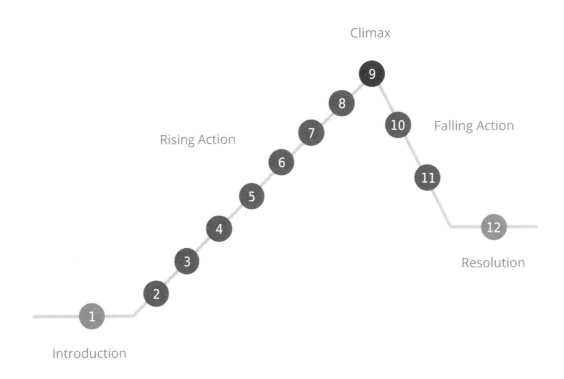

## Introduction

1. Rivers treats Sassoon, who wrote an anti-war Declaration.

## Rising Action

2. Rivers treats many men with mental or physical trauma.

3. Rivers treats Prior for muteness, which then disappears.

4. Prior meets Sarah Lumb and begins dating her.

5. Sassoon meets and mentors Owen, a fellow poet.

6. On holiday Rivers saves Burns from committing suicide.

7. Rivers is offered and accepts a job at a London hospital.

8. Sassoon decides to return to France if he can.

## Climax

9. Rivers witnesses Yealland's electroshock treatments.

## Falling Action

10. Rivers rethinks his duty in light of his anti-war principles.

11. The Board lets Sassoon return to France.

## Resolution

12. Sassoon returns to the front.

# Timeline of Events

**July 1917**

A London newspaper publishes Siegfried Sassoon's Declaration against the war.

**Summer 1917**

Sassoon is sent to Craiglockhart War Hospital to be treated for mental instability.

**Summer 1917**

Officer Billy Prior, mute because of war trauma, arrives at Craiglockhart as Dr. Rivers's patient.

**Summer 1917**

Rivers's dream shows his conflict about causing pain and sending soldiers back to the war.

**Summer 1917**

Prior's parents visit him at Craiglockhart and speak with Rivers.

**Summer 1917**

The poet Wilfred Owen arrives at Craiglockhart and is befriended by Sassoon.

**Summer 1917**

Prior meets Sarah Lumb, a munitions worker, and they go out together.

**Summer 1917**

Rivers hypnotizes Prior, who remembers his traumatic war experience.

**August 1917**

Prior and Sarah have sex for the first time.

**September 1917**

Rivers takes a three-week rest leave from the hospital.

Autumn 1917

Rivers returns from his leave, and Sassoon decides to return to France.

November 14, 1917

Rivers leaves Craiglockhart to work at the London hospital with Dr. Yealland.

November 24, 1917

Rivers witnesses Yealland's electroshock treatment of traumatized soldiers.

November 26, 1917

Sassoon is discharged from Craiglockhart to return to the front.

# Chapter Summaries

## Part 1, Chapters 1–3

### Summary

### Chapter 1

Chapter 1 begins with Siegfried Sassoon's open letter, or Declaration, opposing World War I. Dr. W.H.R. Rivers, a well-known psychiatrist at Craiglockhart War Hospital, near Edinburgh, Scotland, is reading the letter, which its author admits is a "willful defiance of military authority." The letter says soldiers are being sacrificed for an "evil and unjust" war. Sassoon is a well-known poet who was a military officer in France. His Declaration had been published in a British newspaper. The military has decided to send Sassoon to Craiglockhart for "treatment" of mental instability rather than respond to or allow wider publication of his anti-war Declaration.

Rivers wonders if Sassoon is, indeed, shell-shocked, or suffering from stress because of his war experiences. Rivers discusses the case with Dr. Bryce, another Craiglockhart psychiatrist. Bryce is worried about the publicity the hospital will get when Sassoon arrives. As Rivers is aware, by claiming Sassoon is "suffering from a severe mental breakdown," the military does not have to take his anti-war letter seriously. Rivers tells Bryce he'll accept Sassoon as a patient.

Sassoon is on the train heading for Craiglockhart. He had expected to meet his friend the writer Robert Graves, but Graves never shows up. Sassoon cannot stop thinking about Graves. Sassoon remembers telling Graves he wrote his Declaration to publicize his opposition to the war. He hopes the anti-war letter will lead to his court-martial. Sassoon wants a court-martial because it will further publicize his anti-war message and, he hopes, turn the public against the war.

Sassoon recalls an earlier trip to the seaside with Graves, where they discussed Sassoon's Declaration. At the time Graves warned Sassoon the military might have him locked up "in a lunatic asylum" to shut him up. Sassoon is fearful as he remembers his awful hallucinations of corpses. Graves implores Sassoon to realize the military will never court-martial him, because they don't want the publicity it would generate for his anti-war ideas.

Rivers waits for Sassoon at the hospital. He reads the citation on the medal Sassoon received for his bravery in battle. He wonders why Sassoon has thrown the medal away. Rivers thinks about Sassoon's true state of mental health. Rivers is a bit uneasy because "he wanted Sassoon to be ill" to avoid court-martial. He thinks about how he might treat Sassoon if the letter is purely a statement of his conscience and principles and not a manifestation of mental disturbance. Sassoon arrives at the hospital in a taxi.

### Chapter 2

Rivers is meeting with Sassoon for the first time. He notes Sassoon has no outward signs of trauma such as tics or a stammer. Sassoon tells him, rather sardonically, his Medical Board review was rigged. Rivers says that's a serious charge and asks Sassoon to describe the questions he was asked at his Board hearing. Sassoon admits he'd told the Board he no longer dislikes Germans—the enemy in the war. This is an enormous change; after a friend was killed in battle, Sassoon went out into No Man's Land either looking for German soldiers to kill or hoping the Germans would kill him.

Sassoon describes some of his more horrific war experiences. Then he describes his nightmares and hallucinations, horrors he sees in his dreams and when he awakes. Once he saw Piccadilly—a famous square in London—"covered in corpses." He sees "men with half their faces shot off, crawling across the floor." Sassoon is not sure if he's shell-shocked. Sassoon then tells Rivers he's not a pacifist; he believes some wars may be justified, but this one is not. Nothing, he says, can "justify this level of slaughter." During questioning by Rivers, Sassoon admits that the dislike he once felt for Germans he now feels for the complacent civilians who prosecute the war but do not make any sacrifices for it.

Sassoon and Rivers discuss the Board's arrangement to send Sassoon to the hospital to prevent him from publicizing his Declaration in a court-martial. Sassoon explains he threw away his medal because he was upset about the war. Rivers says Sassoon is not mad or insane; he just has a "very powerful *anti-war neurosis*." It's a joke, and they both laugh.

Later Rivers sits with Bryce, his fellow psychiatrist, at dinner, and he tells Bryce he can find nothing wrong with Sassoon, whom he likes. Sassoon, Rivers says, just wants "some kind of *limitation* on the [war and killing]."

Sassoon is in the dining hall too, but at a different table. He cannot talk with his table-mates because they stammer so badly. He remembers a particularly harrowing day during the war when mortar bombs fell on the trenches. A man at his table, Ralph Anderson, RAMC (Royal Army Medical Corps), asks Sassoon if he plays golf. Sassoon responds with an enthusiastic yes. They arrange to play one day soon. Then a commotion starts as a soldier begins choking and vomiting. He's hurried out of the dining hall.

Rivers leaves the dining hall to see to the choking victim, David Burns, who is in bed and being cleaned up by VAD (Voluntary Aid Detachment) nurses. Burns is emaciated, and Rivers puts his arms around him to calm him down. Burns's experience of falling into the distended, exploding body of a dead German soldier has rendered him unable to eat or sleep normally. Rivers offers to put a bowl of fruit in Burns's room, and Burns accepts.

Rivers leaves Burns and goes to an outdoor tower at the hospital. He contemplates the ways men like Burns deal with "unbearable experiences." Burns relives his war terror each night and at each meal. Rivers recognizes that Burns's "suffering was without purposes or dignity."

## Chapter 3

Sassoon greets Robert Graves when he arrives at the hospital. After he settles in, Graves meets with Rivers. They discuss Sassoon's condition and the awkward, even dangerous, position he's in with the military brass. Graves admits to being horrified by Sassoon's Declaration, and he worries Sassoon wants to "destroy himself." Graves admits he rigged the Board decision to have Sassoon sent to the mental hospital for a "nervous breakdown" rather than have him face a more dire punishment. And after all, Sassoon is ill with nightmares and hallucinations. Getting Sassoon admitted for a nervous disorder was rather a feat, Graves explains, because some of the Board members did not believe in the existence of shell-shock. But because Sassoon was such a fine officer—he nearly received a VC, or Victoria Cross medal, for his valor—they sent him to Craiglockhart. Graves admits he agrees with Sassoon's

opposition to the war—at least "in theory." Graves wonders if Lady Ottoline Morrell (1873–1938, an aristocratic patron of the arts) and Bertrand Russell (1872–1970, a philosopher and sometime pacifist) influenced Sassoon's decision to oppose the war and publish his Declaration. Graves is not worried about himself; he thinks he'll be able to go home to Litherland, a town near Liverpool, England.

After Graves leaves, Rivers opens the envelope Graves had given him. It contains three of Sassoon's anti-war poems. The first describes the horrors of trench warfare and the agony of wounded soldiers. The second, titled "The General," castigates the powerful men, the "incompetent swine" who perpetuate the war. The third poem, "To the Warmongers," describes the horrific memories of the dead and dying Sassoon will carry with him throughout his life. Rivers is surprised the poems deal with remembering the war. Most soldiers at Craiglockhart repress the memories of their war experiences. Rivers's job as a doctor as he sees it is instead to help traumatized soldiers remember these repressed war memories. Rivers realizes he'll have to approach Sassoon's treatment differently. Rivers wonders if writing the Declaration had a somewhat healing effect on Sassoon.

As he starts his rounds Rivers runs into Campbell, a soldier who's gotten Sassoon as a roommate. Campbell asks Rivers if Sassoon is a German spy because of his first name—Siegfried. Rivers reassures him he's not.

## Analysis

Sassoon's Declaration in opposition to World War I opens the novel and expresses his conviction that the war is inhumane, "evil and unjust," and perpetuated by powerful men who benefit from it. Sassoon knows the soldiers who sacrifice their bodies, minds, and lives are doing their duty, but they are paying in blood for the "political errors" made by the warmongers. Sassoon has written the Declaration because he could no longer ignore his conscience, which forces him to protest strongly and publicly against the slaughter.

The military Board exercises its power by locking Sassoon away in something akin to a "lunatic asylum" to silence him. Sassoon, a well-known published poet, is denied the power of self-expression because he might persuade others to oppose the war. The military Board is determined to suppress Sassoon's statement of principle and to use their power to propagandize in favor of their war. Sassoon feels it is his duty to use his limited power as a well-known poet to try to end it. The Board was "going to certify" Sassoon as insane, which might have kept him in an asylum for the duration of the war. Yet Rivers recognizes Sassoon's Declaration "was motivated less by a desire to save his own sanity than by a determination to convince civilians that the war was mad." The Declaration was principled, not self-aggrandizing.

The inhumanity of the war leads inevitably to the trauma the soldiers endure. This is evident in the experiences remembered by Sassoon and repressed by David Burns. Sassoon's visions and Burns's disabilities arise from their war experiences. Both men—like all the soldiers being treated at Craiglockhart—are experiencing shell-shock, which was the term for such trauma at the time. Graves's experience testifying for Sassoon before the Board confirmed the military's indifference to the soldiers' trauma: "I got the impression they didn't believe in shell-shock at all. As far as they were concerned, it was just cowardice." Rivers, however, assures Sassoon that "hallucinations in the half-waking state are surprisingly common ... [are] not the same thing as psychotic hallucinations." Rivers exhibits compassionate understanding of the symptoms of trauma, or "war neurosis," something the military brass seem unwilling to do.

Sassoon's Declaration is the clearest statement of conscience and principle in the novel. Sassoon is well aware the Declaration could be dangerous for him. Yet he is determined to face the consequences of his outspokenness. He had to write the Declaration because his conscience no longer permitted him to ignore the agony and outrage of this misguided war. He heeded his conscience and acted on principle to do something he hoped might help end the fighting and the needless suffering it caused.

Sassoon strengthens his principled stand when he says he's not a pacifist. He's impelled to act and speak out because "this [war doesn't] ... justify this level of slaughter." Limiting his opposition to this particular war shows that Sassoon's Declaration is based on principle and conscience, not on seeking publicity or "conscientious objector" status. The latter would label Sassoon a dishonorable coward.

The other main character, Rivers, is conflicted by duty and conscience. Throughout the book he struggles with two opposing forces: his compassion for the soldiers in his care and his duty as a military doctor and officer. Sassoon presents

a particularly difficult case because he wants to be court-martialed to publicize his views, but Rivers's job is to cure him so he can go back to the front. Rivers's conscience and principles are constantly challenged by the requirements and expectations of his professional position.

Graves brings up another aspect of principle and doing one's duty in the war. He agrees with Sassoon's assessment of the war but insists "You can still speak up for your principles ... but in the end you do the job." Graves's attitude raises several questions. What is the good of "speaking up for your principles" if the speech is suppressed because those in power don't like the principles? Further, if duty always trumps principles—which can be mentioned but not acted on—what is the point of having them?

When Rivers puts his arms around the terribly distressed Burns, he is, in effect, challenging the prevailing attitudes toward manliness. Rivers is not afraid to show compassion and caring to another man, even if most British men of the time would condemn such behavior. But Rivers is a man whose empathy and compassion live near the surface, and he easily and unselfconsciously expresses these feelings when soldiers are in need of comfort.

The symbol of the color yellow appears here. Burns is described as a "thin, yellow-skinned man." The yellow color comes from exposure to the chemicals in TNT, an explosive used in World War I. Yet the color yellow also represents cowardice when applied to soldiers. The color also references the determination of military brass to define shell-shock, or trauma, as cowardice, as revealing the soldier as a coward or yellow-belly.

Sassoon's first poem uses the image of trenches to express the indifferent and cruel power of the military. An officer strides through a tunnel until he trips over a huddled soldier in the dirt. He kicks the soldier to awaken him ("Wake up, you sod!") but then sees the horrible face of the long-dead soldier. The connection between trenches and death is clear. They do not shelter the men as much as they imprison them in the struggle and often hold them there long after death. It is a particular horror to encounter death in the midst of one's own life, unthinkingly.

The second poem, "The General," refers to the powerful men—the "incompetent swine"—who started the war and who are determined to see it continue. The general is so deluded or indifferent he "smiles [at] the soldiers ... most of them dead."

The poem refers to Arras, a bloody battle in France in April 1917 between the British and Germans.

"The General" references Sassoon's idea about the "old men," those in power who sit comfortably at home, promote the war, and callously ignore the suffering they cause. Sassoon says they are the men who "sit around in clubs cackling on about 'attrition' and 'wastage of manpower.'" Sassoon is contemptuous of these soft, safe, and complacent warmongers, saying, "You don't talk like that if you've watched [soldiers] die."

The third of Sassoon's poems, "To the Warmongers," is a rhyming anti-war poem that unflinchingly describes the trauma of the battlefield and the writer's experiences there. Its imagery is of horror, pain, and trauma. Yet the last stanza is ironic in its description of the dead as emblematic of glory and pride; that's how the warmongers who have never been there view them. Sassoon punctures that callous viewpoint by revealing that he cannot glorify the carnage: "the wounds in my heart are red,/ For I have watched them die."

# Part 1, Chapters 4–5

## Summary

### Chapter 4

Rivers is listening to his patient Anderson, a surgeon, describe his terrible and strange nightmares. Anderson tells Rivers he can no longer abide the sight of blood. His horror of blood began in France when he failed to notice and treat a serious wound on a mud-covered French soldier. The soldier bled to death. Anderson is seriously concerned not only about his traumatic nightmares but about how he will make a living for himself and his family. How can he be a doctor when he can't stand the sight of blood? Rivers attempts to analyze Anderson's nightmares, hoping he can free Anderson from his fear and enable him to practice medicine again. Anderson's hospitalization and his questionable future compromise his sense of manhood and so complicate his future.

Sassoon and Graves go for a swim in the hospital pool. Graves notices Sassoon's scarred shoulder, and Sassoon sees the shrapnel wound high on Graves's thigh. As he swims, Sassoon

thinks Graves is luckier than another soldier in a hospital who'd been wounded in the groin.

Rivers returns to his room to find Sassoon waiting for him. Sassoon has slept well. The pair discuss Graves's role in having Sassoon sent to Craiglockhart. Sassoon feels Graves overemphasized Sassoon's mental breakdown to get him sent to the hospital. Sassoon feels that emphasizing his breakdown allows Graves not to do anything about the war that he, too, opposes.

Sassoon compares himself to Richard Dadd, a painter who murdered his father—one of the powerful men he thought "deserved to die." Sassoon discusses his childhood and youth, explaining how his father and brother died. He describes a privileged but lonely childhood. Rivers asks Sassoon why he "joined up on the first day," and Sassoon explains how enthusiastic he was about the war in 1914. During their talk Rivers realizes Sassoon "can't bear to be safe," which somewhat embarrasses Sassoon. Rivers says that if Sassoon keeps up his protest he may be kept safe in England for the duration of the war and he "might find being safe while other people *die* rather difficult." Sassoon replies angrily, "Nobody else in this *stinking* country seems to find it difficult. I expect I'll learn to live with it."

Outside, it's a rainy day, but Burns takes the bus into Edinburgh anyway. He gets off in the countryside and walks through a ploughed field. As he reaches the crest of a hill he realizes he should find shelter from the rain. But the mud on the field drags at his footsteps, reminding him of the mud in combat. He sits and rests under a tree. He starts walking again and brushes against something slimy that scares him. He sees it's a dead mole hanging from a tree branch. Burns looks up and sees the whole tree covered with suspended dead animals "in various stages of decay." In panic Burns runs from the tree and back into the field. As he runs, he hears Rivers's voice tell him "If you run now, you'll never stop." So Burns turns back toward the death-bedecked tree. Slowly he unties each dead bird and small mammal from the tree. He arranges their small corpses in a circle on the ground around him, and he sits in the circle's center. He thinks they all can naturally dissolve into the earth. When he realizes he's dressed—and thus denied this natural decaying—Burns takes off his clothes. He remains seated in the center of the circle as it gets darker and colder.

Burns's long absence from the hospital raises concerns among the staff. Rivers and Bryce even consider calling the police to conduct a search. But at six o'clock in the evening Burns returns, "trailing mud, twigs, and dead leaves." A nurse sees Burns entering his room. She scolds him but gets hot water for his bath. Before he can bathe, Burns starts to fall asleep. He thinks of the wood and himself circled by the dead animals. "There is no reason to go back," he thinks. "[I] could stay here [Craiglockhart] forever."

When Burns wakes up, Rivers is sitting by his bed. Rivers does not scold Burns for disappearing; he's only glad he came back. Burns realizes he'd come back to the hospital for this—for Rivers and his empathy.

## Chapter 5

Rivers makes his nightly rounds and meets Prior, a new patient who has terrible nightmares and is mute. Rivers finds Prior lying on his bed reading. When Rivers questions him about his nightmares, Prior answers in the only way he can—by writing his reply in large capital letters on a notepad. Prior claims not to remember his nightmares. There is nothing wrong with Prior physically, so Rivers knows his muteness arises from trauma. Rivers tries to engage Prior by writing, but eventually Prior gets disgusted and writes, "NO MORE WORDS."

Sassoon is at the train station where Graves is about to leave. Sassoon admits he's frightened about coming so close to a complete mental breakdown. Sassoon leaves Graves and begins walking back to Craiglockhart. He finds he hates every civilian he passes on the street. As he leaves Edinburgh and strolls along the bucolic lanes back to the hospital, Sassoon is reminded of the battlefront in Arras, France. Everything had been destroyed by bombing. It was, he thinks, a Golgotha, the place where Jesus Christ was crucified, whose desolation was unimaginable. Sassoon then realizes that what Rivers had said about his hating safety was wrong. Some part of Sassoon longs for safety and delights in the comforts of the hospital.

At the end of a long day, Rivers gets ready for his nightly bath. As the bath fills, Rivers wonders what to do with Prior, whose terrible nightmares keep his roommate sleepless. Once immersed in the bath, Rivers becomes suddenly furious at the "overcrowding and the endless permutations of people" at Craiglockhart. Before he goes to bed, Rivers thinks Sassoon is wrong to attribute selfish motives to those who support the war. Rivers must support the war effort because of his job, but he'd selfishly prefer to be back at university doing research.

Rivers awakens early from a startling nightmare, which he writes down as soon as he's awake. The nightmare is about research he'd done on Henry Head when they were at Cambridge University. As in life, in the dream Rivers was testing Head's sensitivity to pain. Rivers is using various instruments to map protopathic areas—skin sensitive to strong, crude sensory stimuli—on Head's arm. Then the nightmare changes, and Head is holding a scalpel to test pain sensitivity in Rivers. Head is making an incision in Rivers's left arm when Rivers wakes up from the dream.

Rivers analyzes the nightmare's meaning. The basic subject of the dream mirrored the research on nerve regeneration he and Head had been doing in a London hospital. As part of the research, Head had offered himself as an experimental subject. Rivers had severed one of Head's nerves, and then the two researchers charted the process of regeneration. Early in the process, protopathic sensitivity was restored, as determined by very painful experiments done on Head. Even small pinpricks caused him "extreme" pain. Causing pain distressed Rivers, yet he did not stop the experiments.

Further analysis reveals to Rivers that his nightmare was about his "distress at causing pain." The "fear and dread" he felt on awakening reinforces this interpretation. Rivers becomes aware of the conflict between doing one's duty—carrying out the painful experiment—and his innate "reluctance to cause pain." In the dream as in his work at Craiglockhart, there is a conflict between Rivers's duty and his compassion and kindness. Rivers recognizes that his "belief that the war must be fought to a finish ... and his horror that such events as those which had led to Burns's breakdown should be allowed to continue" have created an insoluble internal conflict for him.

Rivers realizes "almost all [his] dreams ... centered on conflicts arising from his treatment of particular patients." Further, his treatment methods are experimental. By having soldiers remember their war trauma, Rivers is causing them pain. Then Rivers realizes the experiment he's conducting is one of eliciting emotion from the soldiers through his caring for them. He understands he's going against society's dictate that men must "repress feelings of tenderness for other men" and that it's unacceptable for a man in psychic pain to cry. By calling forth traumatic memory in his patients, Rivers is freeing their emotions. Rivers recognizes he is "redefining what it meant to be a man," but he is also freeing his patients from fear and crippling trauma.

# Analysis

In Chapter 4 Anderson dreams he's wearing a woman's corset. Anderson interprets this dream image to mean he has been emasculated by "being locked up in a loony bin." Anderson's identity as a man has also been undermined by his "extreme horror of blood," which makes him incapable of again taking up his profession of medical doctor. He's terribly worried about how he will support his wife and children. Being unable to provide for a family makes him feel unmanned. Rivers, however, tries to help Anderson overcome his terror of blood, which emerged while he was working as a doctor at the front, so he can reenter his profession. In one part of his dream, Anderson was wearing a "post-mortem apron." This worries Rivers, who thinks Anderson may feel so emasculated that he's thinking of committing suicide.

Burns too exhibits a less extreme form of emasculation when he's sitting in the center of the circle of dead animals. After removing all his clothes, Burns "cupped his genitals in his hands, not because he was ashamed, but because they looked incongruous, they didn't seem to belong with the rest of him." In his stressed-out state, Burns does not feel his manhood is really a part of him. Burns wants to be one with the dead animals, to decay with them into the earth in a natural way, but somehow his identity as a man must be disconnected from that. In some way Burns must feel unmanned to become one with the dead animals surrounding him.

In Chapter 5 Rivers's nightmare clearly reveals how thorny the issue of manliness is for himself, for his patients, and for Englishmen in general. Rivers understands his dream was about "the distress he felt at causing pain," such as the pain of recalling war trauma. He encourages his patients to remember and fully feel their painful, repressed memories of the war to free themselves from the physical or mental disabilities brought on by trauma. But revealing emotions and feelings is something British society thought of as unmanly and unacceptable. Rivers wisely understands that "feelings of tenderness for other men were natural and right"; by accepting these feelings in his patients, Rivers is going against his—and their—upbringing. Yet he knows it's the only true way to cure his patients.

Prior's muteness represents his inability or unwillingness to speak about the horrors he experienced in the war. He communicates only in writing to indicate that he doesn't remember anything about his wartime experiences or his

shattering nightmares. His muteness is a manifestation of Prior's trauma, but he also seems to use it as a way to hide himself from other people—especially Rivers. When he finally can speak, Burns replies to each of Rivers's gentle inquiries with claims of ignorance or with sarcasm.

Anderson's breakdown occurred when he failed to heal a soldier covered in mud. The thick mud hid the wound that made the soldier bleed to death. Mud was an indicator of death for that soldier. Ever since that incident, Anderson associates mud with blood and death, and he's had a traumatic aversion to both blood and mud.

As Burns treks through the field toward the tree, his feet are sucked down by mud, reminding him of the wartime feel of slogging through mud. After his slog Burns seems to be ready to die. Again, mud indicates, or represents, death. After moving through the mud and removing his mud-covered boots and clothes, Burns is ready to die along with the animals he has placed on the ground. He has been through death (mud) and has now left it behind. He is naked and unmuddied, so he can accept a natural death. In some ways, passing through the mud and the experience in the circle of dead animals has freed something deep inside Burns.

Sassoon stammers a bit when he's talking to Rivers about Graves's testimony before the Board. Yet once Sassoon launches into his scathing attack on the "old men" who perpetuate the war, his stammer largely disappears. He cites a patricide he seems to admire for making "a list of old men in power who deserved to die." In many ways Sassoon feels an equal—if not homicidal—hatred for the "old men" who support the war. The symbol of the "old men" as reviled warmongers is clear here. When Rivers asks Sassoon if he'd find it hard to be safe while others die in the war, Sassoon notes that no one else seems to find it hard; it's likely Sassoon is thinking primarily of the "old men" who have sacrificed nothing for the war.

# Part 1, Chapters 6–7

# Summary

# Chapter 6

Prior's muteness disappears when he wakes up shouting in the middle of the night. He tells Rivers this mutism "comes and goes," and it may come back again "when [he] gets upset." Prior and Rivers discuss their lives before the war. In conversation Prior is smart and clever, yet he still claims he doesn't remember traumatic incidents during combat. He also refuses to talk about his pre-trauma war experiences and his nightmares. Prior states, "I don't think talking helps. It just churns things up and makes them more real." To which Rivers responds, "But they are real." Prior has no reply. Rivers feels Prior's resistance is leading nowhere; he thinks it indicates Prior's unwillingness to be treated and to recover. Prior says he wants to recover, but he only wants treatment that involves hypnosis.

Before Rivers will consider hypnosis he wants Prior to share some of his wartime experiences. Prior describes "standing up to my waist in water in a dugout in the middle of No Man's Land being bombed to buggery." Prior spent days packed in with other soldiers, immersed in muddy water while the Germans lobbed shells at the dugout nonstop. After more than two days in the dugout, Prior is carried to the CCS (casualty clearing station) behind the lines.

Sassoon and Rivers are having a session. Sassoon suggests others must think his Declaration was influenced, even directed, by well-known pacifists of the era, such as Bertrand Russell or Edward Carpenter (1844–1929; poet, philosopher, and pacifist). Sassoon denies any pacifists influenced the letter. Sassoon had visited Carpenter, who was an activist for gay rights, and the conversation becomes awkward. Their discussion of Carpenter's book *The Intermediate Sex* (1908) eases the atmosphere. They talk about how greatly the book influenced the lives of many men. Sassoon says he was also influenced by Robert Ross (1869–1918), the Canadian journalist, pacifist, and art dealer, who was the lover of Oscar Wilde (1854–190), the brilliant wit and playwright who was jailed for his homosexuality.

Rivers is catching up on some paperwork when he's told Mr. Prior wants to speak with him. Mr. Prior is Billy Prior's father, and he's visiting the hospital with Mrs. Prior. Rivers and Mr. Prior discuss Billy's condition. Mr. Prior had not wanted Billy to enlist and reproaches him for joining up to get away from his boring job as a shipping clerk. Mr. Prior approves of Billy leaving his old job but blames his wife for making her son too

ambitious—or trying to rise above his station. Mr. Prior then says Billy was bullied as a young boy. When Billy cried about it, his father slapped him hard and shoved him out the door. Mr. Prior believes "You've got to toughen [boys] up." He admits bullies beat his son badly at times. One day, however, Billy had had enough, and he "half bloody murdered" his tormentor. Still, Mr. Prior says he's not proud of his son being an officer in the army because it's too high class for a boy from a working-class background. As he leaves, Mr. Prior says he'd be a lot prouder of his son if he'd been shot instead of shell-shocked.

Rivers continues working on his reports but is then interrupted by the arrival of Mrs. Prior, Billy's mother. She apologizes for her husband. Rivers notes her voice is "carefully genteel," supporting Mr. Prior's notion that she has ambitions to rise above her class. She admits she's very proud of Billy and says her husband could "never accept that Billy was different." She notes that Billy and his father were not close, even though Billy was "all for the common people."

Rivers is interrupted again by the arrival of Mr. Broadbent, a patient at the hospital who insists he's a captain in the military. Broadbent asks for leave to visit his ailing mother and wants Rivers to put in a good word with Bryce.

Rivers meets Billy Prior after dinner. Prior is wheezing badly from asthma. They talk about Prior's parents. Prior says his father is "a bar-room socialist" who "uses his mother as a football" in the house. Rivers takes Prior to sick bay for his asthma. Rivers is worried about how Prior will be during the night.

# Chapter 7

Sassoon wakes up in the middle of the night to the sound of screaming. He reflects on the previous day when his Declaration was read aloud in the House of Commons—the British Parliament. He shakes when he thinks of the other patients at Craiglockhart—their disorders terrify him.

Rivers visits Prior in sick bay. Rivers is relieved to find Prior breathing more easily. Prior admits to "wanting to impress" Rivers, although he thinks that's pathetic. Then Prior tells Rivers he wishes Rivers acted more as himself rather than as featureless wallpaper who doesn't react personally to his patients' confidences. Prior shows Rivers he's reading *The Todas*, a book about the Toda people of southern India, which Rivers wrote in 1906, when he was doing anthropological studies in Asia. Prior and Rivers discuss the sexual mores of the Toda people. As their conversation gets testy, Rivers again asks Prior to talk about his war experiences. Prior begins talking about snobbery. He admits he encountered snobbery among the officers in France, but it was "not more than I have [encountered] here." Prior describes the qualities he lacks—the right schools and clothes, hunting and riding skills—and his army training in riding like a gentleman. He thinks the whole thing's rubbish. He describes the absurd but fatal punishment three men suffered simply for being caught smoking. They were sent into battle without weapons; two died and the survivor was flogged the next day. Prior bristles at the false notion that there "are no class distinctions" at the front. He describes some of the benefits officers get that lower-class soldiers do not—for example, more time with prostitutes. When Rivers presses Prior to talk about his nightmares, Prior again insists he can't remember. Prior once more mentions his desire for hypnosis, but Rivers explains it might cause problems such as memory loss. Rivers leaves with a sense of foreboding about Prior's hypnosis.

Rivers and Sassoon discuss official reaction to the reading of the Declaration in Parliament. Sassoon begins to stammer when he rages against an item in a newspaper about a 17-year-old soldier killed in action. Sassoon says his roommate Campbell has more coherent ideas about the war than Haig (Field Martial Douglas Haig: 1861–1928). Rivers then offers to nominate Sassoon for the Conservative Club, a club for upper-class men, which pleases Sassoon. Sassoon also says he's sending for his golf clubs so he can play. Rivers thinks it a splendid idea. Rivers then questions Sassoon about his childhood and upbringing.

In his report about Sassoon, Rivers describes Sassoon's 1914 accident, when training a horse, and his bout of trench fever in 1916, when he was sent home to recover. On his return to France, Sassoon was shot in the shoulder in April 1917 and returned to Britain to recover. Rivers notes the magnitude of the slaughter has always horrified Sassoon and led him to believe the war is unjust. Rivers then writes about Sassoon's Declaration against the war, which led to his being sent to Craiglockhart. Rivers insists Sassoon is "intelligent and rational," with no signs of depression. Rivers briefly describes Sassoon's childhood, his illnesses, his going to the right schools, his love of hunting and cricket, and his talent as a poet.

Bryce, Rivers, and the other Medical Officers (MOs) are meeting to discuss their patients. Bryce tells Rivers he gave Mr. Broadbent leave to see to his ailing mother. When the topic turns to Sassoon, Rivers defends his seeing Sassoon three times a week because he "shan't be able to persuade him to go back in less [time] than that."

## Analysis

Billy's father, Mr. Prior, is an exemplar of the British idea of manliness. Mr. Prior seems not to like his son, nor is he proud of him. Probably like many Britons of the time, he thinks being in a mental hospital is shameful. Billy Prior mentions his father would have preferred it if he had been shot ("had a bullet up the arse"). Mr. Prior is also keenly aware of social class. He feels Billy's mother encouraged Billy to have ambitions above his working-class roots. This both angers Mr. Prior and makes him somewhat jealous of his son. Mr. Prior has bullied his son and believes men should be tough or else "there's plenty [of people] to walk over you." Mrs. Prior admits Mr. Prior never understood Billy, who was different from his father and did not fit the stereotype of what a working-class man should be. Later Billy says his father beat his mother, which was likely viewed as acceptable—or at least tolerated—manly behavior.

In a significant theme in the book, manliness blends with homosexuality in the case of Siegfried Sassoon. Sassoon hints he is gay by referencing his acquaintance with openly gay men (Edward Carpenter, Robert Ross). However, Sassoon does not come out to Rivers, because at the time homosexuality was a crime punishable by imprisonment. The discussion of Carpenter's book *The Intermediate Sex* reintroduces the concept of emasculation. Rivers says, "In the end nobody wants to be neuter." Rivers wants men to be men, whether gay or straight; he objects to the emotional repression imposed on men by British society.

Manliness coincides with class consciousness and snobbery, both rampant in British society at the time. Mr. Prior says Billy "should've stuck with his own" and limited himself to acceptable working-class ambitions. He is not proud his son became an officer; this elevates Billy above his class. At the beginning of Chapter 6, even Rivers reveals his class bias, noting Billy has "a Northern accent, not ungrammatical," as if anyone from the north of England is expected to be uneducated, rather illiterate, and stupid. It's possible the often-contentious conversations between Rivers and Billy Prior are due partly to their class differences. For example, when Rivers asks Prior how he fit in with other officers at the front, Prior asks, "You mean, did I encounter any snobbery?" "Yes," Rivers replies. "Not more than I have here," Prior says. Clearly in this scene both Prior and Rivers are acknowledging snobbery and class differences.

Class is dealt with far more casually when Rivers and Sassoon speak together. They are kindred spirits in their privileged upbringing. Rivers offers to help Sassoon get into the posh Conservative Club for rich Tories—political right wingers. Sassoon thanks Rivers and then offhandedly says he's sending for his golf clubs so he can play in his spare time. Rivers thinks it's a grand idea. Both social clubs and golf clubs are the province and privilege of the upper classes at that time, war or no war, and are things both Rivers and Sassoon take for granted.

The rich and powerful men who support the inhumane war are also from the upper class. In talking about class bias in the military, Prior says, "For the first time I realized that somewhere at the back of their ... *tiny, tiny* minds they really do believe the whole thing's going to end in one big glorious *cavalry charge*." Prior is talking about the rich proponents of war who are so out of touch they nurture absurd, unrealistic, and romantic notions about the conflict. Yet anger about the war and the warmongers also may be a connecting tissue between men of different classes. Sassoon, too, is furious at the rich warmongers who perpetuate the slaughter. Even though he is of the upper classes, Sassoon is outraged when he reads about a 17-year-old boy killed in action: "He wasn't old enough to *enlist*. And nobody gives a damn [that he's been killed]."

Outrage at the inhumane war intersects with the duty to fight it. Prior is ruefully sarcastic when he puts on a private-school upper-class accent to tell Rivers, "The pride of the British Army requires that absolute dominance must be maintained in No Man's Land at all times." It's a farcical—if lethal—delusion. Prior describes the days he spent packed into a flooded dugout under constant bombardment by the enemy. He did his duty to fulfill absurd and inhumane commands from the "warmongers" who have no idea of the suffering they are causing the men.

Rivers, too, is challenged by his sense of duty, and perhaps attraction. At the after-dinner staff meeting to review cases, a colleague questions Rivers about his intense attention to Sassoon. Rivers defends his three-times-a-week meetings with Sassoon, saying this is the only way to "persuade [Sassoon] to go back" to fight. Yet the reader knows Rivers is conflicted

about doing his duty in this arena. Like Sassoon, he feels the war does not justify the massive death and suffering it causes. His defense before his colleagues is just one side of the issue of duty Rivers struggles with.

# Part 2, Chapters 8–9

## Summary

### Chapter 8

Prior tells Rivers about his experience fighting on the front lines in France. He tells how soldiers get ready for an attack; how they calm themselves before they're ordered to go "over the top." Prior recalls the April 14 attack, when many soldiers are killed as they emerge from the trenches. Others are mowed down by enemy fire as they charge "toward a line of machine guns." Prior insists the whole operation was a ridiculous event. Rivers says Prior relates events with "inhuman detachment." Prior describes the open ground as pitted and "covered with ... writhing" bodies, "like a fish pond that's drying out." Prior is sent flying by a shell blast, and he wakes up in a crater with other soldiers. At that time Prior could speak. The men leave the crater after dark and return to their line. Rivers probes for more information, but Prior insists he remembers nothing after this. The session ends in feelings of antagonism.

Sassoon is cleaning his golf clubs when a young soldier approaches carrying five copies of Sassoon's book. The soldier stammers as he asks Sassoon to inscribe his books. The soldier introduces himself as Wilfred Owen and says he writes poetry too. Sassoon mentions his brother died at Gallipoli (in Turkey, 1915–16; a foolhardy Allied attack and bloodbath that killed 46,000 and wounded 250,000). Owen is intimidated by Sassoon's good looks and "aristocratic" bearing. To keep the conversation going, Owen praises Sassoon's poems. The pair discuss poetry and writing. Then the topic turns to religion and pacifism. Owen says a true Christian would have to be a pacifist even though he, like Sassoon, is not. The conversation turns to the trenches and the horrors of the war. They are lost in their memories of war until Sassoon says he's late for golf. Before he leaves, Sassoon asks Owen to bring him some of his poetry to read. Owen is thrilled at Sassoon's attention and interest.

Anderson and Sassoon are in the bar of the golf club after their game. Anderson apologizes for almost violently assaulting Sassoon on the green, but Sassoon shrugs it off. At the club they talk only about golf, never the war. Anderson especially does not want to delve too deeply into his trauma and his feelings about the fighting. Anderson thinks about Sassoon's Declaration, resenting its implication that anyone who disagreed with it is callous. Anderson doesn't believe he is callous, even though he thinks the war should be fought to victory.

Prior is in a pub in Edinburgh. He gets hungry and goes into a café, where he notices a group of women. The yellowness of their skin makes it clear they work in a munitions factory. The women are gossiping and laughing, talking about clothes and men. As Prior eats, a young woman in the group, Sarah, begins talking to him. Prior is attracted to Sarah's beautiful hair. He asks her out for a drink, and she accepts. Sarah Lumb tells Prior about her job making detonators. She works long hours, six days a week, but the money is good. Sarah is a "Geordie"—a native of Newcastle in northeast England—but she came to Edinburgh for the work. Her former boyfriend was killed by poison gas released by his own side (during a battle in Loos, France, in 1915). She and Prior talk about whether there can be love between a man and a woman. She doubts it; Prior says he doesn't know. They leave the pub and go for a walk, ending up in a church graveyard. Prior starts to touch her but she pushes him away. Prior is tired of this game. Sarah allows him one kiss and agrees to see him again the next Sunday. Prior realizes it's so late that the gates to Craiglockhart are locked for the night.

# Chapter 9

Rivers explains to Prior why he's being punished for being out so late the night before. Prior is grounded for two weeks, which he thinks is too severe. Yet he'd crudely insulted members of the staff when he'd been let in. Rivers ignores Prior's complaints and begins to question him again about his war experience. Prior repeats he has no memory of what happened to him after the battle on April 14. Prior asks Rivers to explain why mutism is less common among officers than "private soldiers." Rivers thinks it's because "the consequences of [an ordinary soldier] speaking his mind are always going to be far worse than they would be for an officer." Officers, he explains, are more prone to stammering, a physical symptom that may mask psychological trauma. When Rivers suggests officers are

smarter than regular soldiers, Prior is furious. He attacks Rivers by asking why he himself stammers. Rivers is taken aback but explains his stammer likely comes from some internal conflict. Prior is so astute and insightful in his analysis of Rivers's stammer that Rivers cuts the session short.

Rivers takes a walk around the hospital grounds before his next appointment. He sits on a bench and watches two patients using scythes to cut the grass. They remind him of Death, whose scythe cuts down the living.

That evening Rivers is compiling a list of men to be boarded, or assessed for their fitness to return to duty. Rivers dislikes this task, as his recommendation to the Board might determine whether a soldier lives or dies. Prior enters Rivers's room and apologizes for their earlier confrontation. They begin talking about Prior's nightmares, which he says are "muddled up with sex." Prior, like many men, is struggling with the enforced celibacy of life in the hospital. Rivers suggests they try hypnosis now.

When Prior is under hypnosis he seems to wake in a dugout. An officer calls the soldiers to "Stand to." The trench is filled with mud. Prior has "first trench watch," and he begins patrolling it. He chats with two soldiers cooking a makeshift breakfast. It's a relatively quiet day with little bombardment. Suddenly Prior hears a shell screaming toward them; then he realizes it's exploded inside the trench. He hears men screaming. One soldier has been blown to bits; he's barely recognizable. The two breakfasting men met the same fate. Another soldier, Logan, opens a sandbag, and Prior begins shoveling "soil, flesh, and splinters of blackened bone" into it. He's almost finished shoveling when Prior looks down and sees an eye on the ground. He holds it in his palm, and then offers it to Logan with the words "What am I supposed to do with this gob-stopper?" Logan "tips the eye into the bag." Logan and Prior spread lime over the area where the men were killed. Prior begins to feel numb. Back in the dugout Prior admires the complex movements he sees in the faces of soldiers who are speaking. Prior tries to speak but cannot. Logan takes Prior to the casualty clearing station. Prior is cheerful, even exultant and feels no fear. At the station Prior sees a soldier with a back or spine injury who is beyond help. Prior sits on a bench and clearly recalls what happened to the two dead soldiers.

While Prior is under hypnosis, Rivers watches "the play of emotions" on his face. When Prior is brought out of his trance, he asks angrily, "Is that all?" Yet soon Prior's rage turns to bewilderment, and he begins to cry. Prior grabs Rivers and begins butting him in the chest—the closest he can come to human contact. Prior then describes what he'd seen under hypnosis. He admits he'd been convinced he was to blame for the death of the two soldiers in the trench. He describes the chaos of the lines and a deadly incident involving friendly fire. A British soldier had fired on his own troops and thus had experienced "the worst thing"—harming your own men, even inadvertently.

Rivers returns to his room and realizes he's extremely stressed. Perhaps he needs some leave. In the bath Rivers remembers a patient he'd treated, John Layard. Layard was like Prior in his deft wit and insight into Rivers—in his "outrageous frankness." Layard had said he viewed Rivers as his "male mother," an expression Rivers dislikes. Rivers recognizes that he's "touched by the way in which young men ... [felt] like fathers" to their troops. They worried about them as poor, single mothers worry about their children. Rivers contemplates the paradox of the war, which is "the most brutal conflict" but sets up a caring relationship between officers and their men in a "feminine" way.

## Analysis

Inhumane war and its resulting trauma are explored in these chapters. Prior seems "inhumanly detached" from the horrors of his experience in the inhumane war. He describes horrific experiences casually and with seeming disinterest. He says that when he and the soldiers went "over the top" they moved "In a straight line. Across open country. In broad daylight. Toward a line of machine guns." He smiles and shakes his head at this, calling it "*extremely* ridiculous." What he describes in the aftermath of a shell exploding in the trench is appalling, but Prior can remember the horror in detail. His offhand way of describing such horrors is a coping mechanism to protect himself from feeling the inhuman horrors of the war. He tells Rivers, "you can make me remember the deaths, but you will never make me feel."

Hypnosis reveals the incident that precipitated Prior's mutism. Prior is in the trench after bombardment. After shoveling soldiers' remains into a sandbag and finding an eye in the mud, Prior's mind snaps and his face becomes numb. He "watches people's lips move" as they speak and finds these movements amazing. But when he tries to move his mouth and face to talk, he realizes that he had no idea "how they combined together

to make sounds." Yet the "worst thing"—the ultimate trauma—leading to Prior's muteness was the idea that he'd been responsible for the deaths of the men who died in the trench. The paralyzing sense of guilt—of having failed in his duty to protect his men—terrified Prior and made him mute.

In their conversation Sassoon and Owen discuss poetry and religion, debating whether a Christian must be a pacifist. The issue is one of conscience and principle, and neither man can accept pacifism as an acceptable response to the war. Yet Sassoon expresses the idea that war may be an eternal and inevitable result of humanity's inhumanity. In France, he says, "at night you get the sense of something ancient. As if the trenches had always been there. You know one trench we held, it had skulls in the side ... like mushrooms. ... It's as if all other wars had somehow distilled themselves into this war ... I seemed to be seeing [the war] from the future. A hundred years from now they'll still be ploughing up skulls ... I think I saw our ghosts." The war is like a cosmic presence, always there, his words reveal. In its unparalleled inhumanity, World War I seems to contain within it all the inhumanity of all wars ever fought or ever to be fought.

Anderson, too, struggles with his principles, conscience, and ideas about the war. Although he has lost his livelihood as a doctor because of his horror of blood, Anderson still believes the war "had to go on." Anderson bridles at the arrogance of Sassoon's Declaration because it makes anyone with opposing principles seem callous. Anderson rejects the idea that his principles make him indifferent to the suffering of others.

Prior says Rivers "will never make him feel," which for Rivers is a precondition for healing and recovery. Rivers's treatment requires men to open themselves to their repressed emotions—a direct challenge to prevailing notions of manliness. After hypnosis has released Prior's repressed emotion, he clings to Rivers as if to a father. Yet once he stops crying, Prior apologizes to Rivers for this unseemly display of unmanly emotion. Rivers tells Prior a mental breakdown is not something one "kind of person" does, implying a weak or unmanly soldier. It can happen to anyone who is under enough stress or who experiences frequent trauma.

Rivers's experience with John Layard, his former patient, evokes uneasy feelings that seem to challenge his manliness. Layard had told Rivers, "I don't see you as a father, you know .... More a sort of ... *male mother*." The remark made Rivers uncomfortable; he "disliked the term 'male mother'" and the implication that nurturing was a female activity, even when it was done by a man—"as if the ability were in some way borrowed, or even stolen from women." Rivers likens Layard's idea to the ancient practice of *couvade,* rituals men performed when their wives were pregnant. Yet in treating his patients, Rivers tries to open them up to emotions British society thought of as feminine. Rivers had often "been touched by the way in which young men ... spoke about feeling like fathers to their men." A horrific war brought out the caring and comradeship British society deemed unacceptable in men. By calling the relationship between officers and their men "maternal," Layard reveals his disengagement from his own emotions and his ability to care for others. The conflict between the call to stereotypical manliness and the necessity of caring contributed to the trauma and breakdowns soldiers suffered.

Wilfred Owen feels intimidated by Sassoon's "aristocratic voice" and "bored expression." Owen is acutely aware that Sassoon is from the upper classes. When Owen approaches him, Sassoon is wearing "a purple silk dressing gown" and polishing a golf club. The reader gets the idea that Sassoon's innate snobbery is toned down during this meeting only because he recognizes in Owen not only a reader but also a fellow poet.

The relationship between Prior and Rivers is shaped partly by the differences in their social class and a hint of Rivers's snobbery. Prior is outraged when Rivers says, "officers [have] a more complex mental life" than lower-class soldiers, which is why they stammer rather than suffer mutism. Prior is an officer, but he rose from the working class. He rages at the idea that the "*gaggle* of noodle-brained half-wits" has "a complex mental life." Rivers says it's "generally true." Yet this assertion, partly due to snobbery, is belied by previous parts of the novel faulting the upper-class "old men" for the chaos, incompetence, and horrors of the war. Even Rivers agrees with this. The question arises: how can he elevate the upper-class officers when a part of him blames such privileged men for perpetuating a war he hates? When Prior attacks Rivers for his snobbery, Prior points out that Rivers also stammers. Rivers is taken aback, but Prior nails him when he says, "If your stammer was the same as theirs—you might actually have to sit down and work out what it is you've spent fifty years trying not to say." Shocked by the truth of this statement, Rivers cuts short the session. From what the reader knows of Rivers, his stammer may arise from "the conflict between wanting to speak and knowing that what you've got to say is not

acceptable." Rivers wants to protest the inhumane war, but his adherence to duty prevents him from doing so.

Prior had a shared class identity with Sarah Lumb, which may be why he's so comfortable pursuing her. Both are working class and speak freely in a dialect that reflects their similar background. The budding relationship between Sarah and Prior involves Prior's first attempt to reach out to make contact—in this case at first just in pursuit of sex—with another person. Human contact is a path to healing and recovery. Prior's psychic healing is also evident in his actions after hypnosis. Prior tries to diminish the emotional weight of what he discovered under hypnosis, saying "It was *nothing,*" but he cannot maintain his detachment for long. Prior breaks down and cries while he butts his head against Rivers's chest. Rivers realizes, "It was the closest Prior could come to asking for physical contact." And it is a breakthrough in Prior's recovery.

Prior's thoughts contemplate the expanding role of women during World War I. He thinks, "[Women] seemed to have changed so much during the war, to have expanded in all kinds of ways, whereas men over the same period had shrunk into a smaller and smaller space." In many ways the war liberated women, who were entering the workforce. Men, on the other hand, were being ground down and trapped in claustrophobic trenches.

# Part 2, Chapters 10–11

## Summary

### Chapter 10

Sarah and her friends are on their tea break at work. They discuss Sarah's relationship with Prior. Sarah is angry because Prior didn't show up for their scheduled date the previous Sunday; she doesn't know Prior was grounded for coming in late the last time he'd been with Sarah. She claims she's no longer interested in him, but she wonders why he never appeared that day. The topic turns to Lizzie's husband. Lizzie is upset because he will be returning home from the front soon. Lizzie is enjoying her peaceful life without her frequently drunk husband in the house. She says, "I don't want him back ... As far as I'm concerned the Kaiser can keep him." The women encourage Lizzie to get false teeth so she can "have a bloody good time" on her own. Sarah and Betty recall that Lizzie's husband used to beat her.

Rivers is with Willard in the hospital. Willard is lying on his stomach in bed. His back is scarred from the pieces of an exploded tombstone embedded in his flesh. Rivers says the wounds are healing nicely, but he insists once again that Willard's injury has not affected his spine—so Willard should be able to walk. Willard, "his jaw stubbornly set" refuses to believe this. Rivers assures Willard he's not malingering, but he says Willard knows why he can't walk. Willard insists he's not a coward who's pretending he's paralyzed to avoid combat. Rivers agrees. Rivers suggests that Willard get dressed for his wife's visit later that afternoon.

Sassoon has arrived at the Conservative Club where he's to meet Rivers for lunch. He feels the ambivalence with which the stodgy old men there view him in his uniform but with his hospital badge. As he sits and waits, Sassoon overhears two old men talking about the war, and he feels "a well-practiced hatred begin to flow" in him. Sassoon thinks about Gordon, a friend and hunting companion, whose name was listed on the day's roster of those recently killed in the war. Sassoon feels "sickened by himself" because "he'd let himself be pacified" instead of returning to France to support the troops fighting and dying there. Sassoon gets up and looks at the portraits of the rich and powerful men lining the club's walls. He misses hunting, and he misses Gordon. He remembers how he "cracked wide open" after being wounded in France.

Rivers arrives at the club, and the men order lunch. Rivers contemplates Sassoon and feels uneasy about what he might have to recommend to the Board regarding Sassoon's fate. Then Rivers recalls Dr. Yealland, who firmly believed men who broke down were "degenerates" who would break down no matter what their circumstances. Yet Rivers knows that if the innate-weakness theory is rejected, "inevitably the war became the issue." Rivers's form of therapy tests the validity of his theory. Treating Sassoon was difficult for Rivers because it made Rivers think about the prosecution of and justification for the war—notions he'd been able to avoid before. Rivers notes how much Sassoon really cared for the men he led in the war.

Sassoon tells Rivers a supposedly amusing story about how the soldiers were taught to use a bayonet. Then Rivers hints that Sassoon might find the waiter attractive. They talk about the death of Gordon, and then Sassoon recounts how a soldier

he knows who was shot in the throat has suffered a "deteriorating mental state" because he thinks he didn't fight well enough in the war. Rivers offers no comment.

Rivers leaves the club, while Sassoon remains to converse with Ralph Sampson (1866–1939), the Astronomer Royal of Scotland. Rivers is rather awed by the great scientist, but Sassoon chats with him easily. Rivers thinks about how many loved ones and friends Sassoon—and those of his generation—have lost in the war. He thinks this is why Sassoon is always looking back to a time when all those now dead were alive and he was not so lonely. It may also be why young men of his generation are unable "to envisage any kind of future." Yet Rivers wonders how he will get Sassoon to give in, rescind his Declaration, and return to the front. Rivers does not want to force Sassoon to return; he wants to convince Sassoon that going back is "the right thing."

Rivers returns and sees Willard and his wife. Willard's wife is polite, but Willard is in a fury at being so impotent in his wheelchair. When Rivers helps Mrs. Willard push the wheelchair up a slope, Willard is enraged and humiliated. Rivers invites Mrs. Willard to his office for a cup of tea.

## Chapter 11

Owen enters Sassoon's room to see the latter reading a letter from H.G. Wells, who might come to visit him. Sassoon gives Owen a poem for the *Hydra*, the hospital publication. Sassoon tells Owen how Rivers had talked about the future at lunch in order to get Sassoon to return to combat. When Sassoon asks Owen what he plans to do after the war, Owen says "keep pigs." Sassoon is astonished, and Owen knows he's being mocked for his low ambition and for being of a lower class than Sassoon.

Owen shows Sassoon some of his poems, one of which is based on a Greek myth about "re-establishing the link between oneself and the earth" as a healthful way of reconnecting with your true self. The two poets have a fascinating discussion about how to reword and rephrase poems to make them more forceful and meaningful. They also talk about how a poet finds his own original voice in his writing. Sassoon likes Owen's poem "Song of Songs" so much that he threatens to withhold his own poem from publication unless Owen agrees to publish this poem in the *Hydra*. Owen is reluctant but finally agrees to publish it anonymously. Sassoon asks Owen to continue working on his poem "The Dead-Beat," and he asks how long Owen has been working on it. Owen says he spends 15 minutes a day writing poems. Sassoon is flabbergasted. Sassoon advises Owen to work on his poems more assiduously. Yet Owen's revelation shows he's a poetic genius. Sassoon and Owen agree to meet each week to discuss their poetry.

## Analysis

Women's lives and their role in the war effort are explored through Sarah Lumb and her friends, the "munitionettes" after Sarah has gone out with Prior. These women are shown to be dedicated, smart, and wise to their self-interest. They've also gained enough independence to be less reliant on men. Lizzie says about her husband being gone to the war, "[It's] the only bit of peace I've ever had ... I don't want him back." Lizzie thinks of reinventing her life; she'll buy false teeth and then "have a bloody good time." The women work hard but take pride in their work and independence. Their yellow-hued skin is a sign of independence and doing their patriotic duty for the war.

Willard's psychosomatic paralysis arises from issues of manliness. Willard insists he has a spinal injury that has made him unable to walk—even though there is no physical evidence his spine is damaged. Rivers understands Willard's need to survive by not returning to fight. But Willard is consumed by the idea that everyone considers him a coward—a man who pretends to be crippled to avoid doing his duty. A man who is seen as a coward is also seen as less than a man. Being in a wheelchair also imposes a kind of impotence on Willard, which further degrades his manliness. Willard says he knows what others think of him: "I can't walk because I don't want to go back," which is "tantamount to an admission of cowardice." Willard is in a torment of conflict between his will to live and his humiliating status as a coward in the eyes of others—or so he assumes.

Rivers thinks about manliness as well when he remembers Dr. Yealland's view of mental breakdown. Unlike Rivers, who sees mental breakdown as arising from the repression of emotional trauma, Yealland views men who break down as degenerates, as men with an "innate weakness," who fail at being manly enough to resist breaking down.

Sassoon is at the upper-class Conservative Club, but he bristles at the aristocratic "old men" who are there. Although

Sassoon is of their class, the rich old men at the club still remind him of the "old men" who support the war. Sassoon feels "a well-practiced hatred" for the men at the club as well as for those aristocrats whose portraits adorn the walls. In a way Sassoon views the "old men" at the club as hypocrites: They glance at his uniform with approval—he's fighting their war—but they feel uneasy about the mental-hospital badge sewn on it. Sassoon may be justified in his hatred of these pampered rich men. They perpetuate the war and the sacrifice of young men like Sassoon, yet they disparage the effects their horrific war has on the men they have sacrificed.

The snobbery of the upper classes also comes into play when Sassoon mocks Owen's plans for raising pigs after the war. Owen is made to feel ashamed of his post-war ambition, and he blushes when he realizes Sassoon is mocking him—most likely because his plan reveals a lower status. Yet in a way, the reader may interpret Owen's plan as being more realistic and sensible than Sassoon's amorphous indecision about what he'll do with his future. The less posh classes are described as being far more practical and realistic than their "betters."

Sassoon contemplates what his future should be. He feels "sickened by himself" and the way his Declaration is protecting him from doing his duty and returning to the front to be with his men. Sassoon is conflicted: If he stands on principle against the inhumane and unjust war, he is "letting himself be pacified, sucked into the comforting routine of Craiglockhart." If he renounces his anti-war principles, he can then sacrifice his safety and do his duty by returning to the front. Sassoon would then be with the soldiers under his command he cared so much about. Rivers understands Sassoon's feelings. He thinks Sassoon's "love for his men cut through [his] self-absorption," but tormented him all the same.

Sassoon admires officers who care deeply for their men. Sassoon describes a soldier he knows, Julian Dadd, whose mental breakdown is getting worse because he feels guilty about abandoning his men and "not doing well enough" for them. Sassoon says Dadd was "one of his heroes" because he cared for his men so much. Dadd, like Sassoon, feels guilty for being in "the loony bin" instead of in the trenches caring for soldiers. Rivers recognizes how much Sassoon loves his men and how hard it is for him to remain at Craiglockhart when other soldiers are sacrificing their lives in his place.

Owen's poem about the myth of Antaeus deals with the concepts of healing and recovery. There is likely a deep truth in its moral: "the way back to health is to re-establish the link between oneself and the earth ... the 'earth' meaning society as well as nature." Owen believes soldiers have been "ungrounded by the war." By reconnecting with nature—or being grounded in, or connected to, their true inner emotions—those who have broken down can start to heal. This reconnection with the earth also reflects and supports Owen's future plans as a pig farmer. Sassoon, on the other hand, remains unanchored in relation to the future. Sassoon jokingly says being "stuck in a dugout" is not his idea of how to regain "contact with the earth."

The developing relationship between Sassoon and Owen is one of comradeship and mentorship. Sassoon helps Owen with his poetry in a way that might be akin to how he helped his men in combat. In both cases one man cares for another.

# Part 2, Chapters 12–13

## Summary

### Chapter 12

Prior visits Sarah and explains to her why he missed their last date. It's the end of August and still very hot and humid. They take a train out of Edinburgh to the seaside. Prior is annoyed it's so crowded there. He resents the fun other people are having; they seem oblivious to the war and the soldiers fighting it. Prior even begins to hate Sarah because she's a civilian. The pair wade in the surf, but Prior notices a storm is coming. People are running off the beach to seek shelter, but Prior asks Sarah to stay. They shelter among some bushes on the edge of the beach. As they huddle together, Prior's hostility wanes, and he begins to feel affection for her. He longs to have sex with Sarah. Prior asks her if she wants to, and Sarah says yes.

After making love, Prior and Sarah rest in contented silence. After a while they brush twigs and sand from their clothes and walk along the coast They go to a pub for a hot drink and some food. Prior is reminded of a soldier who wrote to his wife every week. Prior censored all of his men's letters, which makes Sarah uncomfortable. Prior tells her no one read his letters because he was an officer. Even his CO (commanding officer) did not censor his letters. As they talk Prior begins to distance

himself from her, denying to himself that anything meaningful had happened between them.

## Chapter 13

Burns is waiting to come before the Board for evaluation. Rivers has told him he'll recommend Burns be unconditionally discharged from the military. Members of the Board ask Burns a few questions, especially about his vomiting. While Burns is questioned, Rivers gets up to free a bee trapped behind a window.

Prior is ill with asthma again. He says it is from all the cigarette smoke on the crowded train during the return trip with Sarah. It seems the smoke caused Prior to pass out. Rivers is sending him to sick bay, which he'll have to share with Willard. Prior makes some sarcastic remarks about Willard's psychosomatic inability to walk. Rivers tells Prior he's having a specialist come to examine him for his asthma. Rivers is worried because this is the second time in six weeks Prior has had a serious asthma attack. Prior doesn't want Rivers to recommend "permanent home service." He wants to go back to the front. He says anyone who didn't fight in France will not "count for anything" once the war is over. Rivers asks Prior how he will withstand mustard gas at the front if he passes out from cigarette smoke. Prior says no one at the hospital wants to hear about the realities of war and death.

Prior tells Rivers eventually he would like to go into politics, but he sneeringly adds he doesn't have the high-class education most politicians have. Prior is surprised to learn Rivers didn't go to a fancy college either.

Later Rivers is in his room shaving when a VAD nurse summons him to see Anderson. Rivers finds Anderson huddled in a corner of his room, his teeth chattering. It seems Anderson started screaming when his roommate, Featherstone, nicked himself while shaving. The sight of blood set Anderson off. Rivers sends Featherstone away and cleans the blood from the washbasin. Anderson begins to relax. When Rivers questions him, Anderson admits his horror of blood is as bad as it's ever been. Anderson is tired of thinking about what he can do to earn a living if he can no longer be a doctor.

Rivers goes to see Willard. As Rivers massages Willard's legs, Willard complains he can't stand being in sick bay with Prior, who still wakes up in the middle of the night screaming because of his nightmares. Willard also intimates that Prior is gay, although Rivers says that's not true. When he leaves Willard, Rivers visits Featherstone, who also demands a room change. Like Prior, Anderson wakes up screaming from terrible nightmares, and he vomits frequently. Featherstone's nerves are shot from lack of sleep. River says he'll see if there's a room available after the September Boards.

Rivers continues his rounds, talking to patients. Fothersgill, Sassoon's roommate, is a religious fanatic who talks as if he's from the Middle Ages. Fothersgill, at 43 years old, feels he's too old to serve, a sentiment Rivers understands.

Rivers next attends a meeting of the Hospital Management Committee, which goes off the rails when a patient representative is overcome by his paranoia about the patients being deprived of food. After the meeting Rivers eats lunch and then goes to see Bryce to discuss Broadbent, a patient who got leave from the hospital to go to his mother's funeral. Broadbent's dissembling became apparent when his mother visited him in the hospital. Broadbent now faces a court-martial. Rivers sees patients for the rest of the afternoon. He's somewhat heartened that several of them appear to be improving.

Rivers is so tired he goes to bed soon after dinner. He's awakened at two o'clock in the morning by chest pains. It seems to be a panic attack brought on by stress, but the symptoms last until dawn. Bryce comes to examine Rivers in the morning, and he strongly recommends Rivers take a vacation. Bryce insists Rivers take three weeks of rest leave.

Sassoon visits Owen in his room, and Owen gives Sassoon a new poem. They discuss rewording some lines in the poem to improve its sound and meaning. Sassoon helps Owen pencil in the changes. Suddenly Sassoon freezes and asks Owen if he hears a tapping noise. Owen does not, and Sassoon wonders what it can be. Owen says that maybe it's the wind, but Sassoon does not think so. Sassoon returns to his room and reads. When Fothersgill enters, Sassoon rolls over in bed and pretends to be asleep. Again Sassoon hears a tapping sound, which reminds him of his last weeks in France. His soldiers had been extremely weak and could barely walk. Sassoon remembers how poorly trained by the military many of the men had been. He wonders now how many are still alive.

Eventually Sassoon falls asleep but wakes suddenly and sees one of his soldiers, Orme, standing by the door. He gazes at Orme standing there but then remembers Orme is dead. Sassoon turns his head to look out the window, and when he turns back, Orme has disappeared. Fothersgill is awake, but, when asked, he denies anyone has been in the room. Sassoon realizes he'd better talk to Rivers about this hallucination, which was so unlike his former visions of gory amputees and the war-wounded. Sassoon is convinced this vision was not a nightmare, but he associates it with the tapping; was it Orme tapping? Sassoon goes downstairs to talk to Rivers, but Rivers has already left for vacation. Sassoon's wan image in a mirror reminds him of the day his father left home when Sassoon was five years old. Sassoon realizes he now views Rivers as a father figure.

## Analysis

At times Prior intensely resents civilians who are enjoying themselves and who know nothing about the sacrifices British soldiers are making in their name. Prior nurtures a deep hostility toward civilians who seem oblivious to the inhumane war and the trauma suffered by those soldiers who are sacrificed to it. At one point, he even hates Sarah for the same reason.

Prior mocks the British class system when he describes to Sarah why officers' mail is not read and censored. "They rely on [the officers'] sense of honor. It would be thought *frightfully bad form*" if that happened, he says in a mock upper-class voice. Instead of laughing at his mockery, Sarah responds angrily, saying, "You lot make me sick ... I suppose no one else's got a sense of honor?" She is defending the honor of the working-class soldiers who are in a sense humiliated and distrusted by the officers who lead them—and who read their mail.

Later, while Burns is facing the Board, Anderson and Sassoon are seen rambling off to the golf course, a subtle dig at their pursuit of upper-class pastimes while lower-class men are having their fate decided. Prior sarcastically confronts Rivers's own class snobbery when he throws back at Rivers his own words about "the greater mental complexity of officers." Prior is mocking Willard, an officer, when he asks Rivers how long it will take to convince "that particular specimen of *complexity*" that "it hasn't got a broken spine." Prior never lets references to class go by without a biting, sarcastic retort.

Prior's ambition to pursue a political career also brings up issues of class and snobbery. Prior doubts he has a future in politics because he lacks a degree from a top-tier university.

Rivers disabuses Prior of this notion. Prior is surprised to learn Rivers did not attend one of these top-tier universities. Rivers tells Prior the war, which increases "contact with the working classes," will make things "freer." In other words, Rivers thinks the comradeship among all soldiers fighting the war will reduce class prejudice and snobbery once the war is over.

Prior is keen to return to the front despite his asthma. He likely wants to go back out of a sense of caring for his men and a willingness to sacrifice himself for them. Prior also wants to return because, he says, "Yesterday, at the seaside, I felt as if I came from another planet." Prior cannot fit into the world of civilians. He is most himself with his comrades in arms. Prior explains his alienation with a fierce critique of how civilians sugar-coat the horrors of the war to make it more palatable for themselves.

Another reason Prior wants to go back is that he does not want to be a man who "counts for nothing" because he didn't spend time fighting in France. His—and others'—manliness is judged by how much time he spent fighting in the war. If Prior is given "permanent home service," his masculinity would be compromised.

Sassoon expresses his innate caring for his men in his friendship with Owen. Sassoon is kind and generous in helping Owen with his poetry. Yet Sassoon also finds that in some way he's haunted by the soldiers he'd cared for. Sassoon has an auditory hallucination of a tapping sound. He then has a visual hallucination of Orme, a dead soldier he had led. This vision seems to him to be a totally different type of traumatic experience than he'd ever had before. Sassoon cannot figure out why the vision of Orme appeared to him the way it did. He looks for Rivers to get his insight, but Rivers is already gone. Sassoon comes to understand in his current circumstances that the caring and compassionate Rivers is a father figure for him.

Rivers's patients represent the wide variety of traumas resulting from the war. Anderson has a mental disability. Willard's trauma is revealed in psychosomatic paralysis. War-related nightmares and other symptoms and behaviors make it difficult for soldiers with different types of trauma to room together—a situation Rivers cannot correct.

In the story of Prior and Sarah, Prior is astonished by the yellowness of Sarah's skin, but it does not make him think her any less attractive. Her unnatural yellowness represents Sarah's hard work at the munitions factory, another indication

of the effects on everyday life, extending to women as well. Later the approaching storm makes the air "yellow ... [and] ... sulphurous," an image possibly referring to the war itself; the TNT used in the war turns everything yellow.

Rivers exhibits his kind and caring nature when he gets up at the Board meeting to free a trapped bee. The incident reveals Rivers's compassion—his recognition of suffering—for all beings, as well as his natural impulse to do what he can to relieve suffering. Yet his tireless care is wearing him out. Overwork and stress take a toll on Rivers in various ways, evidenced by his purported heart condition and his stammer.

# Part 3, Chapters 14–16

## Summary

### Chapter 14

Rivers is on rest leave. He's in church listening to a hymn that has become popular since the battle of the Somme, the bloodiest battle of World War I and really the worst in all of history. It took place between July 1 and November 18, 1916, on the Somme River in France, and left one million men dead or injured. Rivers looks around at the stained-glass windows, especially the one showing Abraham about to sacrifice his son, Isaac. Rivers thinks about the powerful old men who demand the sacrifice of soldiers in the war.

Rivers is staying with his brother Charles who raises chickens on his farm. Rivers is awkward with chickens, but is more helpful working on Charles's accounts. Rivers is aware the farm is not doing well financially. Rivers knows he should be writing letters to Burns, who'd invited him to stay a few days at his family's cottage, as well as to Sassoon. When he's done the accounts, Rivers tries to finish his letter to Sassoon. Yet he's sidetracked by memories of his father, who was a priest and speech therapist. Rivers recalls his father trying to rid his son of his stammer. Rivers also remembers visits from the Reverend Charles Dodson (1832–98, an Anglican deacon, more famously known by his pen name, Lewis Carroll, author of *Alice in Wonderland* among other books). Dodson was a friend of the family and a patient of Rivers's father. Rivers remembers outings with Dodson, as well as Dodson's preference for the company of young girls. Another memory involves Rivers's father listening to his son give a talk on Darwin's theory of evolution. The subject infuriated the senior Rivers, but his son was proud of having "forced his father to listen to what he had to say, and not merely to the way he said it." Rivers returns to the letter but has trouble finishing it.

Back at Craiglockhart, Sassoon and Owen are working on a draft of one of Owen's poems. Sassoon has high praise for the latest version of the poem. With Sassoon's support for his work, Owen is gaining confidence and his stammer is getting better. In its current form, the poem is so good that Sassoon offers to help Owen have it published in a journal (the *Nation*) under the now-famous title "Anthem for Doomed Youth."

Sarah is accompanying her friend Madge to visit her lover in a military hospital. His wound is not serious; when it's healed he'll return to the front. Sarah leaves them together to walk around the grounds. She notices a ward in a conservatory at the side of the hospital. She looks inside and sees rows of wheelchairs and figures "who were no longer the size and shape of adult men." Sarah is shocked by the awfulness of the men's injuries. The men stare at her blankly or with fear. Sarah backs out of the building and realizes her presence has only increased their torment. Outside she feels helpless and then angry because these terribly injured soldiers are hidden away, out of view.

Prior awaits his respiratory examination by Dr. Eaglesham. The doctor asks Prior if he's "keen to get back." Prior becomes quietly enraged, but the doctor remains noncommittal. Prior has no idea what the doctor will say to the Board when the time comes. As he leaves, Prior sees Sarah, and she describes the soldiers she saw in the conservatory.

Rivers spends a few days with Henry Head and his wife, Ruth, in Hampstead in north London. Ruth tells Rivers she "rather enjoys ... air raids" over London. They exhilarate her. Then Ruth admits she supports Sassoon's Declaration. Rivers almost apologizes for his responsibility to get Sassoon, like other soldiers, to return to the front. After dinner that evening Rivers and Henry Head talk together. Rivers describes some of the traumas suffered by the men he's treating at Craiglockhart. Then Head tells Rivers there's a job opening, right for him, for a psychiatrist at a military hospital in London. Rivers says he's interested but is not sure he can leave Craiglockhart. He wants to continue working with Bryce. Rivers has three weeks to decide if he'll take the job.

## Chapter 15

Rivers takes the train to Aldeburgh, and an emaciated David Burns is there to meet him. The pair walks along the seaside. When they get to Burns's house, Rivers thinks Burns looks unhinged. Rivers's evening with Burns passes pleasantly. Rivers notes the strong love Burns has for his home county of Suffolk in eastern England. Burns waxes enthusiastic about local craftspeople, and Rivers thinks Burns is acting like a teenager. Rivers understands that experiencing the war does not mature soldiers as is commonly believed. Nothing is mentioned about Burns's breakdown or illness.

The next day is cold and shrouded in mist. Rivers had been awakened during the night by Burns's nightmares. The men walk a path around the marshes. Rivers becomes aware that the town is surrounded by water, with the River Alde on one side and the North Sea on the other. Rivers asks about a small defensive fort (Martello) nearby, and the two men head toward it. It is a stone structure surrounded by a high moat, which appears to be filled with debris brought in during floods. Burns says as a boy he and his friends liked to imagine the horrible ways people might have died by drowning in it.

Rivers goes out to buy some food and is gratified when Burns eats some. Then Rivers excuses himself to work on a paper, "Repression of War Experience," for a presentation at a meeting of the British Medical Association. As he writes Rivers wonders why he accepts at face value Burns's presentation of himself. Rivers chides himself for going along with Burns's suppression of his war trauma. He decides Burns's war experience was not so different from the other men Rivers has been treating. Later the men go to a pub and are regaled with old Suffolk tales by the crusty Old Clegg who's teaching Burns to make flints.

The next morning Rivers sees a storm coming. Burns had slept badly, tormented by nightmares. Burns rises late and goes out to see Clegg, while Rivers stays in to work on his paper. When Burns returns, he asks Rivers to take a walk with him, but Rivers hesitates because of the imminent storm. Burns dismisses the weather even though the fishermen have hauled in their boats. Rivers takes a long walk with Burns. On returning they walk through an area covered with bloody fish heads left by the town's fishermen. Burns "stops dead in his tracks ... with his mouth working." After a while Burns seems to recover himself, but back at the house Burns refuses food as he had at Craiglockhart. Later Burns chatters on almost incoherently.

Rivers would like to talk about Burns's condition, but Burns wants to go to bed early.

Rivers is awakened by what sounds like a bomb exploding. It takes him a few seconds to realize the sound comes from a maroon—a loud, booming rocket used as an alarm or warning to call on needed lifeboats. Rivers hears Burns walking down the hallway, and he decides to join him in the kitchen for some tea. But Burns is not in the kitchen; in fact, he's not in the house.

Rivers goes outside into the storm to look for Burns. Rivers has the idea that Burns may be in or near the tower. Soon he's running through the rain and mud shouting Burns's name. Rivers peers into the moat, but it's too dark to see anything. He gropes his way down into the moat and in the moonlight sees Burns "huddled against the moat wall." Burns is staring and seemingly unaware of Rivers. Rivers gets Burns on his feet. At first Burns's body is rigid, but then it collapses into Rivers who somehow gets Burns out of the moat and back to his house.

At home Burns says he felt like he "couldn't seem to get out of the dream" he was having. Then the boom of the maroon sent him over the edge. Rivers gets Burns into bed, and he sleeps for a while. The lifeboat comes back the next morning. For the first time Burns begins talking of his war experience. He describes having to write death letters to the families of those killed at the front. He talks about an attack—meant to be a diversion—that killed almost all his men. As Rivers listens he understands the trajectory of the trauma, from fear to indifference to unbearable fear. Burns talks for an hour about his war experiences. The men discuss how evil and cruel people can be. Rivers contemplates the way healing often manifests as decay; how degeneration precedes transformation. He wonders if Burns, who has undergone a "complete disintegration of personality," still has the ability to recover.

## Chapter 16

Rivers returns to Craiglockhart on a stormy autumn day. He goes to see Bryce, and they discuss the letter Rivers had sent about the job at the London hospital. Bryce urges Rivers to take the job, as Craiglockhart's future is uncertain. But the military might remove Bryce from this duty, and Rivers can't imagine working at Craiglockhart without him. Later, looking at his appointment book makes Rivers realize how much he likes

working at Craiglockhart. The work gives his life meaning and gives him peace.

In Rivers's first session with Sassoon, the poet again complains about his overly religious and self-righteous roommate. After a while Sassoon begins to tell Rivers about his hallucinations, both aural and visual. When Sassoon hesitates, Rivers tells him about impossible, seemingly supernatural sounds he'd heard as a field anthropologist in the Solomon Islands. The experience was wholly irrational, yet Rivers knows he heard what he heard. He tells Sassoon it might have been an instance of mass hypnosis or even an incident lacking a rational explanation. Then Sassoon tells Rivers about the tapping and the vision of Orme. Sassoon says the hallucinated men he sees have a puzzled expression. He has written a poem about it, which he shares with Rivers. The poem makes Rivers weep. Sassoon tells Rivers he's decided to go back to France to fight. Rivers is pleased.

## Analysis

Rivers contemplates how powerful people demand the sacrifice of the young, not for a specific purpose but merely to exert their power. In church Rivers equates God's demand that Abraham sacrifice his son Isaac with the powerful men of Britain who also seem to demand the sacrifice of the nation's young men. Both demands seem equally meaningless to Rivers. He thinks of the issue as "a *bargain*" common to patriarchal societies: those who are young and able will obey the old and (physically) weak. The powerful but indifferent old men who demand sacrifice while they remain comfortably at home represent for Rivers the unacceptable inhumanity of the war.

The complacency of the British public is maintained largely by hiding the more hideous effects of the war from view. Those in power who prosecute or support the inhumane war make sure the most atrocious effects and traumas suffered by the soldiers are hidden away. When Sarah sees the horribly wounded soldiers in the conservatory, she feels angry they are hidden away. But those in real power, unlike her, refuse to look. When Prior meets up with Sarah, he sees that she "faced [up to the war] honestly," and he admires her for it.

As a young man Rivers had felt happy and "inwardly triumphant" when, despite his stammer, he gave a good speech about Darwin. Rivers vanquished the personal power his father had over him because he'd "forced his father to listen to what he had to say, and not merely to the way he'd said it." This statement seems related to Sassoon and his Declaration. Young Rivers's speech had fortified his self-confidence and reduced his stammer in the same way Wilfred Owen's stammer subsided as he gained confidence as a poet.

Aldeburgh, the town in which David Burns lives, contains many reminders of war, undermining Burns's ability to bring into consciousness the horrors that led to his psychic trauma. The town is described as having "tangles of barbed wire" and is fortified with sandbags—used in France to strengthen trenches. The tower and moat are defensive leftovers from previous conflicts and remind Burns of the "violent deaths ... the bloodthirsty horrors" of war. Burns is still dealing with his war trauma; he has nightmares and is unable to talk about his war experience. Rivers thinks he looks deranged. Yet when Rivers turns to look at the 22-year-old Burns, he realizes that his retreat to his family home in some way helps him repress his trauma because "Burns seemed not to see the wire" or anything else that might remind him of the war.

When Burns and Rivers walk through the area covered with bloody fish heads, the sight brings back the war trauma to Burns, and he "stopped dead in his tracks." Yet a few minutes later, when they're back in the house, Burns "pretend[ed] everything was normal." Burns continues to suppress his trauma, which accounts for the screaming nightmares that shatter his sleep. The booming of the maroon alarm tips Burns into a distressed state. He says, "I couldn't seem to get out of [my] dream." When Rivers rescues Burns from the moat, it's as if Burns's mind is paralyzed.

After the storm Burns releases some suppressed war memories, and Rivers feels there's hope he'll begin to recover. Burns describes the war's relentless traumas, such as the "little diversion" planned by "old men" who were clueless and indifferent to the danger they put soldiers in. When Burns is able to talk about his trauma, Rivers feels he's on his way to healing and recovery. Rivers realizes the process of healing often "mimics deterioration," and "the process of transformation consists almost entirely of decay." Rivers thinks Burns's journey through a psychic hell might now lead to healing.

When he finally opens up, Burns explains his shame at the possibility that he feigned trauma to avoid having to fight. According to the British definition of manliness, a real man is

never afraid and would never admit he wanted to be wounded to avoid fighting.

Rivers and Burns have an insightful discussion about human nature and humanity's capacity for cruelty and evil. Burns references the Bible and Christ's crucifixion, and Rivers says the worst part of the crucifixion is thinking of someone devising this method of death. Inhumanity—whether in war or in life—seems inescapable. Burns quotes the Bible: "The imagination of man's heart is evil from his youth." This quote explains the inexplicable evil of the war and the unimaginable suffering it caused. However, if what Burns says is true, can the war truly be called inhumane, something not human? According to Burns, and the Bible, the human capacity for atrocity is in fact limitless.

Rivers's sense of duty is challenged when he's offered a job at a military hospital in London. He feels a duty to remain with Bryce at Craiglockhart, but he's drawn to the more prestigious hospital, where he'll also have an opportunity to do research. Yet when he's back in his room at Craiglockhart, Rivers realizes that "the work he did in this room was the work he was meant to do, and, as always, this recognition brought peace." Dealing openly with trauma is healing for Rivers as well as for his patients.

Rivers's primary war trauma is the battle between his opposition to the war and his duty to send healed soldiers back to the front. Yet Rivers is pleased when Sassoon says he's going to return to the fighting, somehow feeing it's right for him to do. In this case Rivers's duty to the military and his need to "heal" win out over his principled opposition to the war.

# Part 4, Chapters 17–18

## Summary

### Chapter 17

Ada Lumb, Sarah's mother, is visiting her daughter and giving her an earful about her relationship with Prior. Ada is vehement in warning Sarah "to keep her knees together" because "men don't value what's dished out free." She also wishes Sarah had a more respectable job than the one at the munitions factory. Even working as a waitress in a tea room would be more respectable than factory work. Sarah realizes her mother wants her to be unlike her and have a better life because Ada struggled to bring up two daughters on her own, without a man. Ada has never told her daughters who their father was or what happened to him. Sarah understands her mother's old-fashioned view of male-female relationships in which "love between men and women was impossible." Sarah asks her mother if it's okay for her to bring Prior to their house when he's on leave. Ada is skeptical, but agrees.

Sassoon meets Graves at the club bar. Sassoon says golf is the only thing keeping him sane. Graves is rather snide when Sassoon talks about Owen and his gift for writing poetry. Sassoon reveals that Owen will probably be sent back to the front lines in a few weeks. Sassoon then tells Graves he's decided to return to the war as long as the military sends him back to France. Sassoon refuses to withdraw a word of his Declaration yet hopes this won't stand in the way of his posting to the front. Graves says he thinks Sassoon is obsessed with being anti-war and thus can no longer make plans for the future. Sassoon says he's thought of little besides stopping the war since the Somme battle, where so many troops were slaughtered. He seems to accuse Graves of not caring enough about the enormous number of war casualties. Graves thinks Sassoon's opposition to the war is "not behaving like a gentleman." Sassoon says Graves's argument is "just suicidal stupidity" because the powers that be are indifferent to the fate of soldiers.

Graves tells Sassoon a mutual acquaintance named Peter has been arrested for soliciting sex near a barracks. Graves is so shaken by the news that he's started dating a young woman. He insists he's not a homosexual. Sassoon is amazed to hear that Peter will be sent to Craiglockhart to be treated by Rivers and "cured."

Sarah is trudging to work for the night shift at the munitions factory, which she thinks looks like hell in the darkness. The women in the changing room are chatting together, and Sarah talks with her friends. Lizzie asks Sarah how her mother's visit went, and Sarah says, "I swore I wasn't gunna tell her about Billy [Prior], but she winkled it all out of me." Sarah is angry because her mother hinted she wasn't good enough for Prior, an officer. Sarah describes her mother's attitude as an insulting "What does he see in *you*?" Madge says boys' lack of exposure to females in school and university tends to make them gay or to avoid women and spend most of their time with other men at their club. The women go onto the factory floor and begin their

dangerous work.

Sarah looks around and asks in a whisper where Betty is, since she's not at work. Lizzie says Betty is pregnant, although she's tried nearly every remedy to terminate her pregnancy. Then Betty resorted to a coat hanger but mistakenly punctured her bladder instead of her uterus. Betty has become extremely ill—but she's still pregnant. Lizzie visited Betty in the hospital the day before, and she says Betty is in terrible shape. The doctors treat Betty badly, telling her "You should be ashamed of yourself" instead of being understanding.

It's the evening before the Board meets, and Rivers is making his rounds. He spends extra time with his patients who will up before the Board the next day. Rivers finds Sassoon in his room, but Rivers has no news from the War Office about what they intend to do with him. Sassoon tells Rivers about Peter, the young man arrested for soliciting near a barracks. He says Graves was devastated by the incident. Sassoon tells Rivers that Peter is being sent to a psychiatrist to be cured of his homosexuality. Rivers notes that psychiatric care is better than a stretch in prison. He says prosecution of homosexuals has increased since the war because of the close relationships, some of which develop into homosexual relationships, that develop among soldiers at the front. Rivers shares a rumor about the Germans: supposedly they have a "Black Book" listing the names of eminent Brits whose private lives make their loyalty and support for the war questionable. As a friend of Robert Ross, Sassoon might be vulnerable. Sassoon refuses to conform his entire life to others' opinions in order to save his reputation.

## Chapter 18

Prior is sitting before the Board, but answers their questions with monosyllabic answers. Rivers is concerned because Prior wants to return to the war despite his asthma, which could prove deadly there. For this reason Rivers believes Prior should not be sent back to fight.

Sassoon sits in the waiting room for his turn before the Board. He's been waiting about an hour, and another patient, Pugh, is still in line ahead of him. Pugh is a "living museum of tics and twitches." A freak accident with a grenade at the front had killed all the men in his platoon except Pugh, who's in very bad shape. Sassoon is getting nervous, and he worries he'll miss his appointment for tea later. A soldier with a terrible stammer asks Sassoon what's taking so long with the Board. Sassoon does not know, but he decides to get up and leave.

Bryce and Rivers are sitting on the Board, and they too wonder why they had taken so long with Prior's interview. Bryce tells Rivers, "at least you got what you wanted. In the end," indicating the Board ruled Prior will remain in Britain. The Board makes quick work of Pugh and the stammering soldier, Thorpe, who says Sassoon seems to have left.

Prior had been crying over the Board's decision. Rivers goes up to Prior's room and tries to explain the decision was made because Prior is not fit for combat. Rivers reminds Prior he'd collapsed during gas attack training. Because Prior's problem is now considered wholly physical, he is no longer Rivers's patient. Prior tries to explain to Rivers how ashamed he is of having failed as an officer because he's not returning to the fighting. Rivers tries to comfort Prior by reminding him that he didn't choose home service, the Board forced it on him. So there's no shame in it. He says, "Everybody who survives feels guilty." As Rivers starts to leave, Prior asks if they might stay in touch after the war, and Rivers says, "I'd be delighted."

At dinner Rivers notices Sassoon is missing; he has still not returned to the hospital. Rivers wonders if Sassoon is on a social visit or if he's deserted. Rivers's thoughts are interrupted by an officer who's arguing vehemently against "racial degeneration [and] the falling birth rate" among upper-crust Britons. The officer rails against the over-breeding of the lower classes in relation to the upper classes. Rivers is relieved when dinner is over, and he leaves a message with a nurse to contact him as soon as Sassoon returns.

Sassoon returns very late. Sassoon explains he left because "I was late for tea with Sampson." After making a few lame excuses, Sassoon admits "he couldn't face" the Board. Rivers expresses surprise at Sassoon's cowardly behavior. Sassoon says he's been considering consulting Dr. Charles Mercier (1851–1919; British psychiatrist specializing in forensics and insanity) for a second opinion. Sassoon reiterates he wants to go back to France to fight.

## Analysis

Ada Lumb is most concerned about class—about respectability and gentility in Sarah's behavior. She wants her daughter to act as if she's of a higher class than she really is. Ada even

"switches to a genteel voice" when she speaks to a waitress to pretend she's not working class. Ada's class consciousness tends to be paradoxical and contradictory, and her sense of class extends so far as to chide her daughter for working with *rough* women at the munitions factory. She wants her daughter to have a more respectable job, even if it pays almost nothing. At the same time, Ada criticizes and insults Sarah for going out with Prior because he's an officer, and Ada assumes this means he's too high-class for Sarah. She says Sarah's "a bloody fool" to step out with a young man above her station.

Class affects how women view their rightful role in society. Sarah reflects on Ada's view in which "marriage [is] the sole end of female existence," but love between men and women isn't really possible. For Ada, and perhaps for most women of her class and era, the male-female relationship is one of manipulation to get what you want or need. Love has little or nothing to do with it. Her view of women as suited only for (loveless) marriages is challenged by her daughter's fierce independence and, in her eyes, unseemly employment.

The women's discussion of Betty's pregnancy reveals further indignities and restrictions on women's lives despite their newfound freedom of employment. Betty is forced to try to abort her fetus herself, and she almost dies in the process. In the hospital the doctors treat her with contempt instead of compassion, telling her she should be ashamed of what's she's done. Madge touches on a truth about British society when she explains the male-only schools that upper-class boys go to tend to bring out any latent homosexuality they may have. When they marry—perhaps for appearance's sake—the men are keen on avoiding their wives and instead spend time at their fancy men's club.

The women's work in the munitions factory also highlights the inhumanity and indifference of those who support the war. The women have yellow skin from the poisonous substances they work with. The gas masks they wear do not fit, allowing toxins to enter their lungs. Yet their bosses are indifferent to the danger the women face every day. Sarah thinks, "All the women were yellow-skinned … We don't look human … [we look] like machines." The inhumane war has rendered women as well as men less than human.

Graves says Sassoon, as a gentleman, must keep his word after he agreed to serve. To do otherwise would be "bad form." Graves uses the strictures and expectations of the upper classes to try to convince Sassoon to return to the fighting. To his credit Sassoon dismisses this class-based argument, calling it "suicidal stupidity."

Sassoon's impatience while waiting for his Board hearing—and his departure from the hospital to keep an appointment for tea—likely arises out of his sense of upper-class privilege. When he returns and talks with Rivers, Sassoon even admits to deliberately acting out of petulance, like a rich, spoiled adolescent. Yet the reader learns Sassoon's rather arrogant departure was due partly to his fear of what the Board might decide. He just used his class privilege to avoid having to face it.

Class prejudice—bordering on something akin to racism—is also undeniable in the major who rails during dinner against "racial degeneration." His is an attitude toward class taken to its extreme. His contempt for the working classes and "the [lesser] supply of heroes" produced by the worthy upper classes reveals his extreme snobbish bigotry.

Graves and Sassoon argue about acting on principle versus doing your duty. Graves again says Sassoon has a duty to return to combat. Sassoon understands this, but he's also struggling with how his duty can be reconciled with his principled opposition to a meaningless war. Later Sassoon disagrees with Rivers and asserts his adherence to his principles and his conscience, saying he can't live otherwise and no one else should either.

Graves, like the others, struggles with his homosexuality and the idea of being "manly" in the strictest British sense. Sassoon is less devastated by a soldier's apprehension for soliciting sex at a military barracks, but he too must contend with being attracted to men in a way that surpasses what was then acceptable, and not conforming to British ideals of manliness. Graves has started dating a woman; he thinks this shows he's "cured" of any homosexual feelings he might have had. He tells Sassoon, "I'd hate you to think I was homosexual *even in thought*." Sassoon knows Graves's true sexuality, so he can't think how to respond to this statement.

The tension between manliness and homosexuality is increased by the war, where fighting men often care deeply for one another. In speaking to Sassoon, Rivers says, "you've got this *enormous* emphasis on love between men—comradeship—and everybody approves. But there's always this ... little anxiety. Is it the right *kind* of love? Well, one of the ways you make sure it's the right kind is to make it crystal clear what the penalties for the other kind are." The

encouragement of manly love in combat must be controlled by the threat of prison if it becomes more than comradeship. Caring for one's fellow soldiers is considered by society to be an example of true manliness. Yet if this manliness gets out of hand it must be punished, Rivers explains. Sassoon replies, "What you're really saying is, if I *can't* conform in one area of life, then I *have* to conform in the others. Not just the surface things, *everything*. Even against my conscience. Well, I can't live like that. *Nobody* should live like that."

Prior, too, is distraught about what he sees as the diminishment of his manhood when he's given permanent home service by the Board. He admits he feels shame at not being man enough to fight alongside the other soldiers at the front. Rivers tries to reason with Prior saying, "I do think you should look at the shame [you feel]. Because it's not really anything to be ashamed *of*, is it? Wanting to stay alive?" Yet the code of manliness is so internalized that Prior—like many other men—cannot endure the guilt and emasculation he feels at being excused from combat.

Pugh and Thorpe, who are waiting for their Board hearing, exemplify the physical and mental breakdown soldiers suffer in the war. Pugh has a near-constant "tic and twitch" accompanied by gasps and screams. Thorpe stammers so badly he can barely be understood. Both conditions represent the trauma war inflicts on soldiers and the trauma's physical and psychological manifestations.

# Part 4, Chapters 19–20

## Summary

### Chapter 19

As Prior waits in the dark for Sarah to signal to him from her window, he suddenly feels as if he's back in No Man's Land, dreading the call to leave the trench and go out on patrol. When Sarah turns on the light in her room, Prior begins to climb up the side of the building and through the window. This is the first time Prior and Sarah will make love naked. Before they have sex, Sarah tells Prior she's glad he's not going back to the front. Prior has never told Sarah what happened to him in France, and he needs to keep this secret from her—even though he wants to be known deeply by her. It's a quandary. Yet Prior tells Sarah he loves her, and she says she loves him too.

Sassoon has brought Owen to the Conservative Club where they talk about poetry. Sassoon reads a poem from a poetry book he's brought with him. Sassoon reveals he's part Jewish. They continue talking, and Owen says he's sorry it's their last evening together. Yet they laugh together as Sassoon reads some particularly awful poems from the book. Then Sassoon hands the book to Owen, and Owen sees Sassoon has inscribed it to him. Owen reveals he's only going to Scarborough (a town in northeast England), and he predicts Sassoon will be back in France before Owen gets there. Sassoon says Rivers is leaving the hospital and laments, "I don't look forward to Craiglockhart without either of you." Unlike Sassoon, Owen is not conflicted about returning to the fighting, even though he, too, opposes the war. As Sassoon leaves the club they wish each other well. Owen feels a terrible sense of loss.

## Chapter 20

It's November, and Rivers is getting ready to leave Craiglockhart. He's glad Willard is much better—"he was walking at last." Yet Rivers is unsatisfied because he never made Willard understand why he had been paralyzed.

Rivers spends his last evening at Craiglockhart visiting Sassoon in his room. Sassoon seems to be in a kind of limbo, but Rivers is glad to know Sassoon is writing poetry. As they say goodbye to each other, Rivers reminds Sassoon he'll be back in two weeks for Sassoon's session before the Board.

Rivers finds lodgings in London near the Royal Flying Corps (RFC) hospital. During the air raids on London, Rivers and the other lodgers take shelter in the basement. On nights when he remains in bed, he's often awakened by the shelling.

After starting work with Henry Head at the hospital, Rivers is fascinated by the differences in breakdown between the regular soldiers and officers and the pilots. He finds pilots who control their planes break down less often and less severely than men in observation balloons. Rivers thinks ballooners' helplessness makes their breakdowns worse.

On November 24, one day before he has to return to Craiglockhart for the Board, Rivers feels obligated to accept the invitation of Dr. Yealland at the National Hospital. Yealland wants Rivers to observe his method of treating physical and mental trauma in soldiers. The empty, sterile corridors of the National Hospital feel eerie to Rivers, reminding him of No Man's Land. The swing door at the far end of the corridor opens, and Rivers sees a horribly deformed man crawl rapidly into the corridor. A nurse appears and shepherds the deformed man to bed.

Rivers accompanies Yealland and two junior doctors on their morning rounds. Rivers notes Yealland's intense stare and his "steady, unrelenting projection of authority." On the wards Yealland has little or no personal interaction with his patients. For Yealland the removal of physical symptoms was tantamount to a cure. On one ward, Yealland and company stop at the bed of the deformed man Rivers had seen earlier in the corridor. Yealland says to Rivers, "This one's fairly typical." The soldier had suffered enormous trauma in the war and has numerous physical symptoms, which have resulted in his deformity. Yet Yealland triumphantly announces the man has "no sign of organic disease." Yealland tells the deformed soldier he will get treatment that afternoon to "make [his] back straight" by application of electricity to the spine and back. Rivers is amazed at Yealland's God-like tone of voice. The patient is alarmed and asks, "Will it hurt?" Yealland replies, "I realize you did not intend to ask that question and so I will overlook it." Near the end of the rounds they approach the bed of a mute soldier, Callan, who's been through numerous horrific battles. Callan has already been treated with electricity and hot plates "applied to the neck and throat." Burning cigarettes have been applied to his tongue. Rivers can't believe what he's just heard. When Yealland asks if Rivers would like to witness a treatment, Rivers says he would. Yealland finds Callan's case interesting because he was not cured with a single electrical treatment, as most other soldiers are.

## Analysis

Sarah hints at the issue of manliness when she tells Prior her mother would like him more "if [he] were going back" to the front. Real men fight; disability or illness diminishes Prior's manliness in the eyes of others.

Wilfred Owen expresses soldiers' common feeling of comradeship and caring when he says he doesn't want to leave Sassoon and the hospital, but "the fact is I'd be taking up a bed some other poor blighter needs far more than I do." Owen truly cares about Sassoon—as a friend, poet, and fellow soldier—and he's "afraid to measure his sense of loss" at their parting.

Rivers's approach to trauma is highlighted in his mixed feelings about Willard regaining his ability to walk. Although he's happy for Willard, he's also exasperated by Willard's refusal to associate his disability with his suppressed trauma.

His experience with pilots and ballooners in the London military hospital confirms Rivers's theory about the causes of war trauma and breakdown. The ballooners' helplessness makes them far more prone to trauma than the pilots, who have control over their planes. Rivers applies this understanding to women in peacetime, too; their "anxiety neuroses and hysterical disorders" are caused by their "confined lives." Rivers ponders how society's imposed gender roles cause traumatic disorders in both men and women. Men are manly if they fight wars and face danger; women are feminine if they accept limited lives and powerlessness. This insight gives him much to consider as he imagines his role with all those who suffer as the war goes on.

Sassoon briefly mentions the upper classes' ignorance or indifference to the realities of war and war trauma; he tells Rivers the aristocratic Lady Ottoline Morrell asked him whether he realized that going back to the war would involve killing Germans. The question reveals a stunning degree of ignorance and insensitivity in the public.

Yealland is an extreme example of the inhumanity and indifference of powerful men who play a part in the war and in the lives of soldiers in wartime. Rivers describes him as God-like and impressive in his "unrelenting projection of authority." Yealland treats the traumatized soldiers at the National Hospital as "cases" and barely acknowledges their humanity, let alone their suffering—particularly their psychological suffering. Yealland never asks the soldiers about their mental state. For him, "In every case the removal of the physical symptom was described as a cure." When Yealland stops at the bed of a hideously deformed soldier, his concern is solely with eliminating the physical deformity. Because there is "no sign of organic disease" in these soldiers, Yealland seems to think they're just being too stubborn to abandon their physical symptoms. Yealland treats his patients by hurting them until they can no longer stand the pain and they then abandon their symptoms. He uses electricity, for example, to get his patients to give up their supposed attachment to their physical

symptoms. In one case, he will use electricity on the spine of the highly deformed soldier to get him to straighten his back. Sufficiently long application of electricity and hot plates to the body of a mute, wounded patient will, Yealland believes, convince the soldier to abandon his symptoms.

Yealland uses electricity to restore his patient's health, although he could probably use any other pain-inducing treatment to achieve the same result. Rivers asks "about the relapse rate, the suicide rate" after the initial so-called treatment seems to work. No one can answer him because no one under Yealland cares enough to find out. For Yealland the suffering of his patients is immaterial; he refuses to see his patients as humans whose feelings are legitimate and should be respected. The way Yealland describes his approach to treatment makes his indifference to soldiers' welfare and his inhumanity perfectly clear. He says patients who enter the electrical room have to know "there's no way out except by a full recovery" and notes the last thing they need is sympathy.

Yealland, like some other powerful men in British society, no doubt thinks it unmanly for men to reveal their emotions, especially fear. Even if men do feel fear, they must keep it bottled up inside. When one patient asks fearfully of the treatment, "Will it hurt?" Yealland replies, "I realize you did not intend to ask that question and so I will overlook it." Later when a soldier being treated breaks down, Yealland says, "You are a noble fellow and these ideas which come into your mind and make you want to leave me do not represent your true self." Manliness demands that the expression of any emotion—such as fear—or feeling—even the physical feeling of extreme pain—must always be buried and never revealed. If, as is likely, Yealland subscribes to this dehumanizing definition of manliness, he has no qualms about his inhumane treatment of patients.

# Part 4, Chapters 21–23

## Summary

### Chapter 21

After lunch Rivers accompanies Yealland to the hospital's electrical room, where Callan is strapped into a dentist-type chair with restraints. An electrode is applied to the back of Callan's throat. The current is so strong it "throws [Callan] back with [tremendous] force." Callan is "white and shaking" as Yealland tells him "you must behave as becomes a hero ... you must talk before you leave me." Yealland applies the electrode to the back of Callan's throat repeatedly, for more than an hour. After this ordeal Callan is able to utter the sound "ah." Again the electrode is applied, with Yealland encouraging Callan to say the sounds of the alphabet (bah, cah, dah, etc.). Despite repeated electric shocks, Callan can still only say 'ah'. After an hour and a half of electric shocks, Callan is becoming exhausted. Yealland walks Callan around the room, and eventually Callan makes a run for it, but the door is locked. Again Yealland tells Callan he will remain until he speaks.

Rivers is upset and tense by what's happening in the room. Memories of his stammer invade his mind. Yealland again straps Callan into the chair for the second stage of treatment—"strong shocks to the outside of the neck." As Callan's neck is shocked, Yealland repeats the alphabet sounds. Finally Callan utters "bah," and Yealland is gratified. Callan starts to cry and uses gestures to ask for water, which Yealland denies him until he utters a complete word. Callan is unable to produce a word, and Yealland becomes exasperated, threatening to use a stronger current. Strong shocks are repeatedly applied to Callan's neck until Callan finally begins to utter several different sounds and then, finally, words. Yealland has Callan say the days of the week, the months of the year. Callan is sagging with exhaustion—and possibly pain. Shocks continue to be applied until Callan starts to speak normally. But as he says these words, Callan suffers a spasm that seems to paralyze his left arm. Yealland applies an electrode to the left arm, and the spasm appears in Callan's right arm. The same spasms happen with Callan's left and right leg.

Yealland pronounces Callan cured and asks, "Are you not pleased to be cured?" Callan smiles in response. Yealland says, "I do not like your smile ... Sit down." When Callan is again in the chair Yealland applies electrodes to the sides of his mouth until Callan no longer smiles. Callan then thanks Yealland for curing him.

## Chapter 22

That night Rivers tries to work on his paper, but he's haunted by the day's events. Rivers feels ill, and he attributes this to the confrontation he had with Yealland earlier. Rivers goes out for

a walk on nearby Hampstead Heath (a large park in north London). Yet Rivers can't get the image of Callan and Yealland out of his head. His walk makes Rivers feel a bit better, and he returns to his rooms and goes to bed.

Rivers has a strange nightmare. He's walking down an extremely long corridor like the one at the hospital. The swing doors at the far end swing open and shut "like the wings of an ominous bird." The deformed man he'd seen at the hospital is in the corridor watching Rivers. Then the deformed man quotes a few lines aloud from Sassoon's Declaration. After this the dream changes. The scene is in the electrical room. Rivers has an electrode in his hand and a man with his mouth open is in front of him. Rivers tries to apply the electrode to the back of the man's throat but for some reason he can't get the electrode inside the man's mouth. He tries to force it in, and the man struggles against it. Rivers looks down at the supposed electrode and realizes it's a horse's bit. Trying to force the bit into the man's mouth has damaged his mouth, which is raw and bleeding. But still Rivers continues trying to force the bit into the man's mouth. When the man cries out, Rivers awakes and realizes it was he who cried out.

The horror of the nightmare lingers for Rivers. He understands that the dream imagery is related to Yealland's treatments. Rivers recalls Yealland boasting about a man with a stammer he had cured with his electrical treatments. Rivers is exasperated when this story worsens his own stammer. He thought "whenever he'd hesitated over a word, he'd sensed Yealland calculating the voltage." Now Rivers understand his stammer emerges from an underlying conflict. Rivers thinks the deformed man in his nightmare represents Sassoon because the man had quoted from Sassoon's Declaration. Rivers feels the mood of the nightmare was one "of the most painful self-accusation."

Rivers wonders about the identity of the second man in his dream—the man he was trying to treat with his own electrode. Rivers concludes this man must have represented Prior, who had also been mute when he first arrived at Craiglockhart. Rivers had "dragged a teaspoon across the back of Prior's throat" when Prior first arrived. Rivers had hoped the choking reflex would "trigger the return of speech ... as it sometimes did." Rivers had felt exasperated when this hadn't worked, but he now admits to himself that he'd felt "a momentary spasm of satisfaction" at Prior's choking. Rivers realizes there's no comparison between the suffering caused by his teaspoon and Yealland's electrodes. Yet in the dream Rivers had been in

Yealland's place. The dream mood of self-accusation might be telling him "There is no distinction" between him and Yealland in their roles.

Rivers contemplates the horse's bit in his dream. It is an instrument of control—to force men back into the war. Yet the application of control applied to him, too. Rivers was "locked in [to his role] every bit as much as [his] patients were." Rivers thinks the bit in his dream might also represent "the scold's bridle," an instrument used to prevent a person from speaking. He knows it had been used to silence women and slaves. Yet Rivers senses Callan had been more eloquent in his silence than in his forced speech. Forcing Callan to speak was, in Rivers's eyes, silencing him. Rivers realizes he silences his own patients—from their muteness, stammering, tremors—when he "cures" them with his treatment. Their disability is eloquent in its protest, the loss of the disability silences their human experience of the horrors. Rivers then realizes the man in the chair before him in the dream must be Sassoon, who has abandoned his Declaration against the war to return to the front—something Rivers had encouraged him to do. That is the root of Rivers's self-accusation.

## Chapter 23

Rivers and Henry Head are discussing Sassoon. Head says there's no comparison between Yealland's and Rivers's approaches to treatment. What worries Rivers is Sassoon's "total inability to think about after the war." Rivers thinks "he's made up his mind to get killed." Head says Rivers should therefore recognize that has Sassoon made his own decision to go back to the front.

Head says Rivers has changed; Rivers responds with a story from his anthropologist days on the Solomon Islands. Rivers was with some native Solomon Islanders, and he asked them what they would do if they had some money; with whom would they share it? Instead of answering, they asked him the same questions. As Rivers was unmarried and had no family, he said he wouldn't share the money with anyone. The islanders were "incredulous ... anybody [could] live like that." The islanders began to laugh uproariously because they simply could not understand a society in which this would be reasonable. Rivers realized he understood the Islanders' society as little as they understood his. Rivers found this wonderfully liberating—"the Great White God de-throned." He realized Western culture is not "the measure of all things ... there was no measure." Rivers

says his patients have helped him remove the societal mask he's always worn and helped him become his true self.

After dinner Rivers makes his rounds as he's always done. He spends most of his time with patients who will be facing the Board the next day. These include Anderson, who still suffers from terrible nightmares, and Sassoon. Sassoon has been "keeping his head down" and also working on his poetry. Sassoon says the frequent letters he gets from Owen reveal a type of hero-worship—or perhaps something more. The War Office has told Sassoon no obstacles will prevent him from returning to the war.

The Board meets the next day. It has a new chairman, but no one knows how this will affect its decisions. Anderson is interviewed first. Rivers says Anderson still wants to serve his country, and Rivers recommends he work in an administrative capacity at the War Office. This type of job will also "postpone the moment when [Anderson] has to face the prospect of civilian medicine." Sassoon is the next-to-last interview of the afternoon. Rivers says he's recommending Sassoon for "general service overseas" because he's mentally and physically fit. Sassoon also wants to go back to the front. When other Board members bring up questions about Sassoon's fitness—regarding his anti-war Declaration—Rivers explains that those were Sassoon's past opinions; he feels differently now. But when the Board questions him, Sassoon says he has not changed his opinion about the war. Rivers is somewhat taken aback. Other members of the Board worry Sassoon will foment rebellion among the soldiers at the front. Rivers assures them he won't.

Sassoon comes to say goodbye to Rivers. Sassoon must begin packing. He'll spend a few days in London and at home and then leave for France. Sassoon admits he lied about his nightmares but insists they'll be gone once he's away from Craiglockhart. Rivers tells Sassoon not to take unnecessary risks, and Sassoon assures him he won't. They'll keep in touch.

Rivers returns to his room to finish up some paperwork. He thinks how much he's changed while treating his patients. He's more comfortable with himself and with his growing opposition to the war and the men who perpetuate it. Rivers wonders how Sassoon will be able to manage in France. Fighting at the same time he held strong anti-war beliefs would create a huge conflict in Sassoon's mind—and make it harder for him to kill and to order his soldiers to kill. Rivers concludes that the only solution to Sassoon's problem was for him to be killed, and

Sassoon intended this. Rivers fears that if Sassoon is not killed, he may suffer a severe breakdown from his internal conflict. But he will go back to France.

## Analysis

Yealland embodies the inhumanity and indifference of those who support the war. He uses electrical torture to force the traumatized soldiers in his care to overcome their mental or physical disability. His callous indifference to the human suffering he inflicts is made clear when he says "You must speak, but *I shall not listen to anything you have to say*." Yealland further alienates the human being from his experience when he states, "you do not understand your condition as I do." Yealland believes the traumatic disability is just a manifestation of a soldier's stubbornness and is, therefore, something he can decide to abandon. Yealland's sadistic approach to the patient-soldiers implies that he thinks their disabilities may be a show the soldiers put on to avoid having to return to the fighting. He may also see his treatments as a battle of wills between him and his patients—a battle in which he with his greater strength of will undoubtedly prevails.

Yealland talks to Callan as if his physical disability is a mere nuisance, one the soldier can easily shed if only he wants to. Yealland says "Remember, you must behave as the hero I expect you to be ... A man who has been through so many battles should have better control of himself." Yealland implies soldiers should become hard and unfeeling heroes after enduring numerous battles. Yealland denies real trauma is a natural and predictable result of horrific war experiences, or he at least believes he can overcome that trauma with his strength, which appears to be almost a physical hypnosis achieved by pain.

Yealland's treatment of soldiers dovetails with the official view of British manliness. Yealland parrots the official military line that all soldiers are, at heart, heroes, and that heroism is the true nature of British men. For Yealland, as for British society, no quarter is given for a male who feels or expresses emotion. The denial of emotion no doubt makes it easier for Yealland to justify his sadistic treatment of his patients. If men either do not feel or successfully bury their feelings, then Yealland's view of traumatic disability as a put-on is supported—and his torturous treatment is appropriate. Yealland even presumes to tell the traumatized soldier who he is and what he should be feeling: "You are a noble fellow and these ideas which come

into your mind and make you want to leave me do not represent your true self." Yealland interprets the soldier's desire to escape torture as a betrayal of his true, manly nature.

Rivers accepts manly emotions, and his treatment involves releasing these emotions through memory and speech; for him this is the key to healing. Rivers seems to have a panic attack when he gets back from Yealland's electrical room. His intense emotional reaction arises from revulsion about what he witnessed.

Yealland has denied any human feeling so he can do his duty to support the war effort. He tells Callan, "You will leave me when you are cured, remember, not before ... the time you have already spent with me is not long in comparison with the time I am prepared to stay with you." Yealland will painfully treat Callan for as long as it takes to get him to start "speaking normally." As Yealland understands his duty, painful treatment is necessary and acceptable because it prepares soldiers to return to the front lines.

In contrast Rivers sees it as his duty to help traumatized soldiers bring into consciousness the war traumas responsible for their disability. That Rivers argued—albeit politely—with Yealland about his objectionable treatment method is made clear when Rivers recalls "the confrontation with Yealland" he'd had after witnessing Callan's treatment. Rivers's experience in the electrical room solidifies his commitment to his anti-war principles and makes him question more deeply the nature of his duty to the military, particularly what happens to the soldiers he heals: their reposting to the front lines.

Rivers's internal conflict between his duty and his principles is clearly explained when he analyzes his nightmare. Rivers insightfully recognizes his dream's overpowering mood of self-accusation. Rivers remembers the discomfort he caused Prior when first examining him. Rivers is appalled at the "momentary spasm of satisfaction" he got from choking Prior. Rivers's nightmare contains a horse's bit—a piece put inside the horse's mouth so the rider may control the animal's every movement. The horse's bit symbolizes the torturous control Rivers, as a military psychiatrist, has over patients.

The dream put Rivers in a situation very like the one he witnessed in the electrical room, showing an equivalence between Rivers and Yealland. The suffering each doctor inflicts may vary in degree, but Rivers believes essentially "there is no distinction" between the two doctors. Like Yealland, Rivers "fitted young men back into the role of warrior, a role they had—however unconsciously—rejected." Rivers realizes both he and Yealland are "*locked in,* every bit as much as their patients were" because they both serve the same military system.

The end of Chapter 22 provides a deeply insightful analysis of Rivers's predicament. Rivers questions the validity of healing, since for his patients healing means a return to the front. Rivers also understands that a mute patient's silence is the patient's eloquent way of expressing his internal state and his refusal to participate in the war. By curing soldiers' muteness or stammering, Rivers—like other military psychiatrists—is not releasing the soldiers' inner truth but rather silencing it; their muteness or stammer is "their unwitting protest" against the war. Because Rivers feels most guilty about his efforts to get Sassoon back to the front, he realizes Sassoon probably was the man he was torturing in his dream.

Class, snobbery, and bigotry all play a part deciding Sassoon's fate. In discussing Sassoon with Rivers, Head appeals to Sassoon's manly honor, an idea wed to class snobbery. It is far more shameful for an upper-class officer to act dishonorably than it would be for a man from the lower classes. The whole issue of snobbery and feelings of superiority is exploded in Rivers's story about his experience in the Solomon Islands. Mutual misunderstanding between the British anthropologists and the Islanders teaches Rivers "we weren't the measure of all things" and, in truth, "*there was no measure.*" This experience liberated Rivers from having to wear the mask of class and culture inhibiting his true self. This experience may also be why Rivers is so attuned to the experience of each individual soldier and does not view them as faceless cogs in the military machine.

Rivers's celebration of individuality is crudely countered at the Board meeting by Major Huntley, who expresses vile opinions about "racial degeneracy"—emphasizing particularly Sassoon's part-Jewish heritage. However, Huntley compounds the insult by saying Sassoon is exceptionally fit "even [for] the upper classes" and his "hybrid [part Jewish] vigor" may be an asset in the fighting. Although Rivers may still feel guilty about his influence on Sassoon's decision to return to battle, he tells the Board they should grant Sassoon's request, even though his anti-war principles are stronger than ever. Sassoon's wish is granted by the Board, yet his principles are intact.

After saying goodbye to Sassoon, Rivers reflects on how much he's been changed, or healed, by Craiglockhart. Sassoon and

his other patients have brought Rivers's anti-war principles into the light. He thinks" the sheer extent of the mess seemed to be forcing him into conflict with the authorities over a wide range of issues ... [but] a society that devours its own young deserves no automatic or unquestioned allegiance." Defending their principles in the face of great personal cost—for Rivers his job, for Sassoon his life—has in a sense liberated and to some extent healed both men while leaving them with deep internal conflicts.

# ‘❞’ Quotes

*"You can ... speak up for your principles ... but in the end you do the job."*

— Robert Graves, Part 1, Chapter 3

Speaking with Sassoon, Robert Graves says he believes people who sign up for military service must continue to serve regardless of their war experiences or their principles. Sassoon enlisted to fight for his country, but his war experience made him an anti-war spokesman. Graves says Sassoon can think what he wants about the war but must not act outright on his anti-war beliefs.

*"Nobody else in this stinking country seems to find it difficult [to be safe while others die]. I expect I'll just learn to live with it."*

— Siegfried Sassoon, Part 1, Chapter 4

Sassoon tells Dr. Rivers how he'll feel if he's discharged and sent home to England instead of returning to battle. He is bitter toward the British civilians who have avoided the war—those who are safe at home and give little thought to the horrors their countrymen experience on the front lines. Later Billy Prior will express similar sentiments.

*"In advising [patients] to remember traumatic events ... [Rivers] was, in effect, inflicting pain."*

— Narrator, Part 1, Chapter 5

Dr. Rivers is an essentially kind man who hates to cause others pain. In both his dreams and his waking life, he is plagued by the pain he causes his patients when he forces them to remember unbearably painful war experiences. Yet he does this to heal their trauma.

*"He's mentally and physically healthy. It's his duty to go back, and it's my duty to see he does."*

— Dr. Rivers, Part 1, Chapter 7

Rivers is explaining his role as a military doctor and Sassoon's role as a patient. Rivers's duty is to send soldiers back to battle after they have healed. Sassoon's duty is to return to the front when his doctor says he is ready for combat.

*"You can make me dredge up the horrors ... but you will never make me feel."*

— Billy Prior, Part 2, Chapter 8

Prior is closed off, self-protective, and adamantly opposed to sharing his war experiences with Rivers. Prior says even if he describes his trauma, he will never allow himself to feel the emotion that accompanies it. Prior shuts himself off from feeling to protect his sanity; he's also afraid of revisiting the intensity of his repressed emotions.

*"This most brutal of conflicts ... set up a relationship between officers and men that was domestic. Caring."*

— Narrator, Part 2, Chapter 9

Comradeship and caring among soldiers and officers is an important theme in the book. Dr. Rivers thinks about how living through the most brutal war atrocities strengthens the bonds among the fighting men.

*"The Great Adventure ... consisted of crouching in a dugout, waiting to be killed."*

— Narrator, Part 2, Chapter 9

These are Rivers's cynical thoughts on the idealized image of war. The British military attracts young men into the army by painting the war as a Great Adventure. Rivers notes that the reality is completely different. Soldiers spend most of their time miserably in foul, crowded trenches that often serve as deathtraps.

*"Yealland ... believed that men who broke down were degenerates."*

— Narrator, Part 2, Chapter 10

Rivers is considering the approach Yealland, a fellow psychiatrist, takes to emotionally damaged soldiers. Yealland believes these soldiers are "degenerates" who break down because they're weak. Rivers disagrees strongly. The two psychiatrists' differing views touch on the question of manliness: a "real" man is not supposed to be weak; a "real" man does not suffer breakdowns.

*"If the country demanded that price, then it should bloody well be prepared to look at the result."*

— Narrator, Part 3, Chapter 14

This is what Sarah Lumb thinks after she's seen the terribly disfigured amputee soldiers who are hidden away in a conservatory ward apart from the war hospital. Sarah believes the British public should be made to see what happens to the men they send to war. The men shouldn't be hidden away to protect people from the consequences of war.

*"Nothing can justify this ... Nothing, nothing, nothing."*

— Narrator, Part 3, Chapter 15

Dr. Rivers has this thought after he rescues his patient Burns from the moat where Burns waited to die. Because Burns is so broken, and his attempted suicide has so shaken Rivers, the psychiatrist expresses this unusually strong—for him—anti-war sentiment.

*"You agreed to serve, and ... you've got to be seen to keep your word."*

— Robert Graves, Part 4, Chapter 17

Here again Graves implores Sassoon to do his duty and return to the fighting. Graves appeals to Sassoon's upper-class obligations, telling him he must honor his obligation or others will "say you're not behaving like a gentleman." For upper-class Britons, not behaving like a gentleman is unthinkable, perhaps unforgiveable.

*"You must speak, but I shall not listen to anything you have to say."*

— Dr. Lewis Yealland, Part 4, Chapter 21

Yealland makes this remark to a mute soldier while using electricity to force him into talking. Yealland doesn't think of his patients as human beings who have feelings and ideas worth sharing. The soldier must speak to show he is "cured," but Yealland cares nothing for what he says. Yealland's words encapsulate the inhumanity and indifference of the military toward the anonymous cogs (soldiers) in the war machine.

*"A horse's bit ... An instrument of control ... he and Yealland were both ... controlling people."*

— Narrator, Part 4, Chapter 22

Rivers has a dream about trying to force a horse's bit into a soldier's mouth; he realizes that it symbolizes his job as a military psychiatrist, in which he wields total control over his patients. This realization helps Rivers awaken to his true purpose in the military; he begins to reject the role of inhuman controller.

*"In present circumstances recovery meant resumption of activities ... not merely self-destructive but ... suicidal."*

— Narrator, Part 4, Chapter 22

Here again Rivers is thinking about the true nature of his job as a military psychiatrist. In non-military psychiatry, patients are considered healed when they no longer engage in self-harming actions. In military psychiatry, Rivers reflects, patients are considered healed when they are ready to be sent back to the battlefield—where they may die. Rivers equates this type of "healing" with preparing a patient for suicide.

*"A society that devours its own*

*young deserves no automatic or*
*unquestioned allegiance."*

— Narrator, Part 4, Chapter 23

Dr. Rivers has decided the war cannot be justified; it does too much damage to those who fight it. Rivers feels he can no longer follow military orders without questioning their necessity and their effect on soldiers. His allegiance to the British military is no longer guaranteed.

# 🐦 Symbols

## Mutism and Stammering

Some of the soldiers at the military hospital are so traumatized by their horrific wartime experiences they are unable to speak. Their muteness is a physical manifestation of the inability to process the horror of the things they experienced. Mutism therefore represents the repression of unspeakable, unbearable trauma. It also symbolizes the unspeakably horrendous conditions and suffering of soldiers fighting World War I.

Similarly, stammering is a soldier's physiological manifestation of the inability to confront and talk about his terrible experiences fighting the war. Stammering is not the result of a physical abnormality but rather a psychological trauma so intense it cannot be given voice. Stammering is another representation of the human mind's inability to process the traumatic horrors of war.

## Old Men

In various parts of the text characters express sneering contempt or vicious hatred for the powerful "old men" who started and perpetuate the war. These "old men" symbolize the narrow self-interest, mindless and anachronistic pseudo-

patriotism, and callous indifference of the powerful to the suffering of soldiers fighting at the front, which were manifested in the time of the war in English society.

In this context the "old men" are the politicians, businessmen, and military bigwigs who sent hundreds of thousands of Britain's young men to fight the war. They are seen as not knowing and not caring about the suffering of the troops. World War I had no real cause or purpose to justify its enormous cost in lives lost. "Old men" therefore symbolizes the willful ignorance and utter indifference of the powerful men who were snug and safe at home, to the unimaginable suffering of soldiers in combat.

## Trenches and Mud

World War I was fought from trenches—deep, winding excavations in the earth the soldiers on both sides lived in and emerged from, "over the top," to fight the enemy. As deep furrows in the ground, trenches are symbolic of graves. In fact, they acted as graves for countless soldiers who died in them—from bombs and from diseases that ran rampant in the trenches. Life in the rat- and lice-infested trenches was so harrowing it continued to haunt the soldiers at the hospital.

As parts of the trenches were open to the sky, rain accumulated at the bottom of them. Thus, trenches were often layered in deep mud. In the novel, some soldiers being treated at the hospital walk in, fall in, or are otherwise covered in mud. Mud, too, represents death in this war. Mud was also what covered the continually bombarded "no-man's land" between the trenches of opposing armies. Many thousands of soldiers died in the mud of no-man's land as they charged across it to attack the enemy and, perhaps, gain a few yards of territory.

## Horse's Bit

A horse's bit represents control. At the end of the novel, Dr. Rivers has a nightmare in which he's trying to force a horse's bit into the mouth of a restrained soldier/patient. When he awakes, Rivers understands the symbolism of his dream. A bit is part of a horse's harness the rider puts in its mouth to control the horse. In the context of Rivers's dream, the horse's bit represents an inhuman, even torturous, means of controlling soldiers.

Rivers's recognition of his complicity in controlling mentally wounded soldiers to get them back to the front as quickly as possible is a turning point for him in the novel. He comes to realize he represents and acts in the interests of the powerful men who have control over the soldiers in combat. The horse's bit that so horrifies him in his dream is an apt symbol of this inhumane control.

# Yellow

Yellow is a symbol of the war and how it poisons people both physically and mentally. In society the color yellow represents cowardice. Some of the soldiers at the mental hospital have yellow-tinted skin or eyes. Their mental breakdowns and their yellow bodies seem to reinforce the idea they're cowards—a notion that Rivers emphatically denies. Yet the yellow color marks these men as victims of war.

The women who work in the munitions factory also develop yellow skin from working with the TNT used in combat. The yellow-colored chemical in TNT is now known to cause severe liver disease, and women who worked in munitions factories were often sickened or killed by exposure to the chemical poison. For the munitionettes, having a yellow color was a mark of patriotism, of doing one's duty for the war effort. Unlike its symbolism for soldiers, yellow-skinned women were not stigmatized but rather respected for their contribution to the war.

# 🎭 Themes

# Traumas of Battle

The soldiers being treated at Craiglockhart War Hospital are

suffering the physical or mental effects of the trauma they experienced at the front. The men try to bury the trauma deep within them, terrified to confront it, but it emerges in a variety of different mental and physical disabilities.

During World War I trauma was called shell shock, although some of the military brass denied shell shock existed. They insisted the physical and mental disabilities exhibited by the affected soldiers were merely signs of "cowardice." But Dr. Rivers and other psychiatrists at Craiglockhart understand that the effects of trauma, or shell shock, are real.

The novel explores how the mind and body react to traumatic experiences so horrifying they must be repressed deeply, beyond memory. No matter what type of experience caused the trauma, it manifests in different ways in different men—from mutism to stammering to bodily paralysis and recurring nightmares or hallucinations. The trauma these men suffer, which the author explores with deep compassion, is today termed *post-traumatic stress disorder* (PTSD).

# Waging War for Power

The conditions under which the soldiers fought in World War I were unimaginably horrific. Yet the powerful men who perpetuated the war were indifferent to the effects of these conditions on soldiers. Those behind the war had power over the soldiers and used to it to make sure they continued fighting, regardless of the life-destroying battlefield conditions.

The powerful pro-war factions in the government and the nation saw it as their duty to force soldiers to return, time after time, to the horrors of the front lines. Yet the soldiers themselves also felt compelled to fight by a sense of duty. Soldiers' patriotism was not of the shallow, self-interested variety—the kind motivating those in power. Rather soldiers recovering from traumatic injuries—whether physical or mental—felt it their duty to return to the trenches out of a sense of loyalty to the men still at the front. Not doing one's duty to return to battle meant another soldier might die in one's place; this produced a sense of guilt and responsibility soldiers could not ignore. Their duty and loyalty was to their comrades who continued to struggle on the battlefield, which explains why they felt it was their duty to go back to fight.

Returning to the front lines was a sacrifice for recovering or recovered soldiers. Even though they might have been allowed to remain in Britain, many, like Siegfried Sassoon, freely made the sacrifice to return to the battlefield. The soldiers' sense of solidarity and comradeship with their fellow fighters might result in a relapse of trauma-related illness or in the ultimate sacrifice—death—but they still chose to fight beside their fellows. The theme of manly love and comradeship is strongly implicit here.

## Defining Manliness

The British ideal of manliness was of the "stiff upper lip" variety; it tolerated no show of emotion, for showing emotion was showing weakness. For some powerful men who perpetuated the war, the physical and mental disabilities exhibited by the soldiers in the hospital were signs not only of weakness but of shirking one's duty. These powerful men did not acknowledge that war trauma could cause such terrible disabilities in soldiers who were "real men." Soldiers of the time (1914–18), having been brought up in this emotionally repressed British society, suffered more acutely. They felt they had to suppress the emotions resulting from their trauma, so they could not express and thus release them. Some doctors, parents, and high-ranking military men reacted to afflicted soldiers with scorn or skepticism because they refused to acknowledge or deal with the emotional traumas the men were suffering from.

Soldiers were generally dissuaded from expressing overt love for the men they fought with and who were generally viewed as caring comrades. Officers especially—men like Sassoon—frequently felt love for the men they led and cared deeply about their well-being. Although in many cases this love emerged out of concern for the soldiers' lives and safety, there are in the novel instances in which it is clear this emotion sometimes involves homosexuality. Sassoon, for example, is strongly drawn to men both during and after the war, although there is no hint he is sexually engaged with the men he leads at the front. Owen, too, develops feelings for Sassoon. At this time homosexuality was a crime in Britain, so its expression had to be closely guarded.

For the most part the feelings soldiers have for each other are

those of deep comradery—a sense of loyalty and a willingness to sacrifice oneself to help or save others. Feelings of comradeship were accepted, even encouraged, by British society so long as they did not evolve into an emotional or sexual attachment.

## Conscience and Principle

Some of the characters in the novel are troubled by having to betray their principles in order to continue to fight in the war, Sassoon being a key example. Although he has written a Declaration denouncing the war, he struggles with how his strong anti-war principles fit in with his duty to his fellow soldiers. Sassoon wrestles with the dilemma of acting according to his principles—which would keep him out of an absurd and meaningless war—or according to his conscience—which would have him return to the front to support and care for the troops he leads.

Other characters, too, struggle to align their conscience and principles with the reality of war they must adapt to. Dr. Rivers is torn by his conscience, which tells him many men in his care should not rejoin the war, and his duty, which is to "cure" his patients so they may return to the battlefield. Rivers's principles on the prosecution of the war are confused but become clarified by the end of the book. Some other soldiers described in the novel must also decide whether to act according to their principles and conscience or according to the military rules controlling them.

##  Motifs

## Healing and Change

The road to recovery in the novel takes many forms and leads to different types of change in different men. Rivers is a healer, but he heals in order to send recovered soldiers back to the front lines. Healing occurs for men who suffer from either or both physical or mental illness brought on by their war experience.

The novel explores how different modes of healing lead to changes in both the healers and the healed. Soldiers who experience some degree of healing often have different fates: some may be returned to the fighting, others may return to desk duty or civilian life. Rivers himself experiences a type of self-healing, despite not being physically injured, that dramatically changes his view of the war.

# Emasculation

The motif of emasculation, or the loss of manhood, recurs in several parts of the novel. Some soldiers suffer physical emasculation from wounds to the groin. In most cases, however, the emasculation explored in the book revolves around the loss of agency, or the power to act on one's own behalf.

The soldiers in the hospital are under the complete control of the doctors and nurses, who are themselves controlled by the military. The soldiers are powerless, which itself is a kind of emasculation. British society's notions of manhood intensify the suffering emasculation causes the men. Fighting is manly; being wounded—physically or mentally—and unable to fight is unmanly. Even though the soldiers' wounds come from their service to their country, they are made to feel less than men if they can no longer fight.

The motif of emasculation is strongly tied into the theme of manliness and its corresponding issues of emotion, caring, conscience, sexual identity, and sacrifice.

# Class, Snobbery, and Women in War

During the World War I era—and still to some extent today—British society was highly stratified and class-conscious. People's status was determined by their dialect or accent, their schooling, their parents' jobs, where they grew up, and where they lived as adults. Upper-class Brits generally looked down on those in the middle, lower, and working classes.

Sassoon is the prime example of an upper-class officer who spends his time chasing upper-class pursuits, such as playing golf and lounging at the "club" for upper-class gentlemen.

Rivers, too, is most likely from the upper echelons of society, although he shows compassionate understanding for his lower-class patients.

Note the off-handed, often snide, dismissive, and insulting put-downs the upper-class men in the hospital use so casually to describe those they deem beneath them. Note, too, the privileges and special treatment the upper-class soldiers receive compared with the treatment meted out to "lesser" men.

The women portrayed in the novel are working-class women who labor in munitions factories to both aid the war effort and earn good wages. They are portrayed with truth and appreciative understanding of their class, their worth, and their ambitions and experiences. Although the upper-class men in the book do not interact with lower-class women, the most caring, intimate, and emotional connection is made between working-class characters, specifically Sarah Lumb and Billy Prior.

# ☰ "Dulce et Decorum Est"

Wilfred Owen wrote what many consider the most eloquent and powerful anti-war poem about soldiers fighting in World War I. Its title, "Dulce et Decorum Est," is taken from the first words of a Latin ode by the Greek poet Horace. The words, translated as "It is sweet and right," appear again at the end of the poem, used with brutal irony against those who unthinkingly encourage war.

Dulce et Decorum Est
by Wilfred Owen

Bent double, like old beggars under sacks,
Knock-kneed, coughing like hags, we cursed through sludge,
Till on the haunting flares we turned our backs,
And towards our distant rest began to trudge.

Men marched asleep. Many had lost their boots,
But limped on, blood-shod. All went lame; all blind;
Drunk with fatigue; deaf even to the hoots
Of gas-shells dropping softly behind.

Gas! GAS! Quick, boys!—An ecstasy of fumbling
Fitting the clumsy helmets just in time,
But someone still was yelling out and stumbling

And flound'ring like a man in fire or lime.—
Dim through the misty panes and thick green light,
As under a green sea, I saw him drowning.

In all my dreams before my helpless sight,
He plunges at me, guttering, choking, drowning.

If in some smothering dreams, you too could pace
Behind the wagon that we flung him in,
And watch the white eyes writhing in his face,
His hanging face, like a devil's sick of sin;
If you could hear, at every jolt, the blood
Come gargling from the froth-corrupted lungs,
Obscene as cancer, bitter as the cud
Of vile, incurable sores on innocent tongues,—
My friend, you would not tell with such high zest
To children ardent for some desperate glory,
The old Lie: *Dulce et decorum est*
*Pro patria mori.*
[*It is sweet and fitting to die for one's country.*]

# 📖 Suggested Reading

Axtell, Candice. "Love Between Men." Kansas State U, 2003.

Bowman, Alicia. "Restoring the Balance." Kansas State U, 2004.

Downing, Taylor. *Breakdown: The Crisis of Shell Shock on the Somme.* Abacus, 2017.

Knutsen, Karen Patrick. *Reciprocal Haunting: Pat Barker's* Regeneration *Trilogy.* Waxmann, 2010.

Mullan, John. "Pat Barker's *Regeneration.*" *The Guardian*, 24 Aug. 2012.

Pierpont, Claudia Roth. "Shell Shock." *New York Times*, 31 Dec. 1995.

Westman, Karin, *Pat Barker's Regeneration: A Reader's Guide.* Continuum, 2001.

Printed in Great Britain
by Amazon